# The
# Assignment

by
Dr. Mike Murdock

Albury Publishing
Tulsa, Oklahoma

# The Assignment

*Powerful Secrets for Discovering Your Destiny*
*Dynamic Steps to Accomplish Your Life's Goals*

by
Dr. Mike Murdock

Unless otherwise indicated, all scriptural quotations are from the *King James Version* of the Bible.

*The Assignment*
*Powerful Secrets for Discovering Your Destiny*
*Dynamic Steps to Accomplish Your Life's Goals*
ISBN 1-88008-994-7
Copyright © 1997 by Mike Murdock
P. O. Box 99
Dallas, Texas 75221

Published by Albury Publishing
P. O. Box 470406
Tulsa, Oklahoma 74147-0406

# Contents

# Dedication

I dedicate this book to five special persons who have helped make my Assignment possible, and whose presence in my life I treasure:

To the Holy Spirit, my number one Mentor.

To my mother, my number one inspiration.

To my father, my number one intercessor.

To Jason, my number one son.

And to Ree, my number one protégé.

# Acknowledgments

Every book requires the toil, time and devotion of extraordinary people. Words are not adequate to explain my gratefulness to those who God assigned to work beside me in this tremendous project, *The Assignment*. Though I fear making the mistake of leaving someone out, I do want to acknowledge with great thanksgiving the following people (in alphabetical order) who made this entire labor of love possible:

Frank and Beverly Berry, my closest friends for more than thirty years, whose belief in me and tireless efforts of support are helping many of my dreams come true.

Walt and Pam Bolinger, whose continuous stream of encouraging words never ends.

J. Konrad Hölé, whose example as a protégé is unrivaled.

Martha MacDonald, whose treasured friendship and conversation inspired my focus to author this book.

Marcus Maranto, whose editorial assistance and enthusiasm kept me motivated hour after hour.

Merlene Marsh, whose enthusiasm for wisdom has been proven over the countless hours she has typed the numerous drafts of my many manuscripts.

My brothers and sisters, whose unwavering confidence in my life and my Assignment is appreciated greatly (Barbara, John, Flo, Deborah, Kaydonna, and David).

Chris Ortiz, whose graphic capability is only surpassed by his prophetic motivation in my life.

Keith Provance, who believed in my Assignment as an author long before I realized it myself.

Iris Smith, whose proofreading revealed more mistakes than I care to admit.

The staff of the Mike Murdock Evangelistic Association, whose excellence in serving is an example to the world — particularly Matti Cook-Smith, my secretary, without whose remarkable tenacity and unbelievably long hours this book would never have been completed. I am also very grateful to my other precious staff members: Elaine Aldridge, Carole Bryan, Alice Cabrera, Tim Childress, Susan Costin, Laura Coulter, Maudie Coulter, Willie Coulter, Loren Davalos, Tim English, Que English, Clint Hall, Karis Hall, David Hodgens, Zaydee Crespo-Hodgens, Marie King, Cindy Kipling, Merlene Marsh, Kevin Matheny, Rebecca McCoy, Monica Melgar, Sergio Melgar, Michael Palmer, Pam Schultz, Laura Thurman, and Todd Voitel.

Pat Vanlandingham, whose endless hours throughout the night allowed us to make the deadline for this whole project.

Bobby White, my loyal friend who constantly looks to lighten my burdens in his dedicated assistance of my ministry.

Steve and Rebecca Williams, whose love and gifts have helped make my home a beautiful haven of rest.

And, Janice Winters, my legal counsel, whose confidence in my Assignment has been a great encouragement.

# Introduction

If you are a Christian, God has an Assignment for your life that will put you in the right place at the right time with the right group of people to fulfill His purpose in your life. But for many, God's Assignment is illusive. Too many of God's children live in a lifestyle of constant failure and futility because their lives are out of focus to the purposes and plans of God.

If Satan can keep the Christian blinded and out of focus to his or her life's Assignments, he can keep them in a lifestyle of failure and strife. But even more importantly, he can bring pain and failure to the heart of God. That is why I have written this book.

As you read the following pages, you will discover the hopes and desires God has always had for your life. You will also discover some of the devices Satan often uses to keep us "outside" of God's Assignment. And you will be encouraged to help others discover God's special Assignment for their lives.

For those who may want to use this book as an aid to daily devotions, I have written thirty-one Assignment Facts, one for each day of the month to give you daily direction.

But whether you read one chapter in its entirety every day, or read them at a different pace, it is my fervent prayer that your relationship with God will increase one hundredfold because of my Assignment to write, *The Assignment.* And that God's purposes and plans will soon unfold in your life.

Mike Murdock

# FACT

# 1

## EVERYTHING GOD CREATED WAS CREATED TO SOLVE A PROBLEM

### YOU ARE NOT HERE BY ACCIDENT

Did you know that God created you to solve a problem? Why did you buy a car? Because it solved a transportation problem. Why do you watch the news each evening on television? It solves an information problem. Why did God create you? To solve a human problem.

- Mechanics solve *car* problems.
- Dentists solve *tooth* problems.
- Lawyers solve *legal* problems.
- Mothers solve *emotional* problems.
- Accountants solve *tax* problems.
- Christians solve *human* problems.

God created the prophet Jeremiah for a special time and season. And because God is no respecter of persons, it is the same with you.

*...for thou shalt go to all that I shall send thee, and whatsoever I command thee thou shalt speak. Be not afraid of their faces: for I am with thee to deliver thee, saith the Lord.*

Jeremiah 1:7,8

## CREATIVITIY IS THE SEARCH FOR SOLUTIONS

> Every part of you has an Assignment.

Let me illustrate: In large gatherings of the past, speakers could not be heard clearly. So microphones and public address systems were created. Eyeglasses were created for those who have difficulty seeing. And a host of other creations have been devised to serve practical needs.

In the same way, every part of you has an Assignment. There is a problem for you to solve. Your eyes have the Assignment of seeing. Your ears solve the problem of hearing.

- Your eyes *see.*
- Your ears *hear.*
- Your hands *reach.*
- Your feet *walk.*
- Your mouth *speaks.*
- Your nose *smells.*

But what are you to do with all these faculties? It is up to you to discover your Assignment and to give yourself totally to it. Because if you don't do it, nobody will:

> *Let every man abide in the same calling wherein he was called.*

1 Corinthians 7:20

## EVERYTHING IN CREATION HAS
## A SPECIFIC PURPOSE

Everything God creates has a specific purpose. It solves a problem. That is why God created us. He wanted a love relationship. He wanted to be chosen, pursued, and treasured. So He created Adam. But the solving of that problem gave Adam a problem: he needed human companionship. So God created Eve:

> *And the Lord God said, It is not good that the man should be alone; I will make him an help meet for him...And the Lord God caused a deep sleep to fall upon Adam, and he slept: and he took one of his ribs, and closed up the flesh instead thereof; and the rib, which the Lord God had taken from man, made he a woman, and brought her unto the man. And Adam said, This is now bone of my bones, and flesh of my flesh: she shall be called Woman, because she was taken out of Man.*
>
> Genesis 2:18,21-23

But once they were together Adam and Eve had a problem! Who would take care of them in their old age? To solve this problem, God gave them children:

> *Lo, children are an heritage of the Lord: and the fruit of the womb is his reward. As arrows are in the hand of a mighty man; so are children of the youth. Happy is the man that hath his quiver full of them: they shall not be ashamed, but they shall speak with the enemies in the gate.*
>
> Psalm 127:3-5

> *And God blessed them, and God said unto them, Be fruitful, and multiply, and replenish the earth, and subdue*

*it: and have dominion over the fish of the sea, and over the fowl of the air, and over every living thing that moveth upon the earth.*

Genesis 1:28

So you see, Adam's wife and children were to be a solution to his problem:

*Thy wife shall be as a fruitful vine by the sides of thine house: thy children like olive plants round about thy table. Behold, that thus shall the man be blessed that feareth the Lord.*

Psalm 128:3,4

But we must never forget that mankind was created for a much higher purpose than that of mere problems. God put man on earth for His good pleasure. We were created to make Him glad:

*Thou art worthy, O Lord, to receive glory and honour and power: for thou hast created all things, and for thy pleasure they are and were created.*

Revelation 4:11

You were not only created to be a solution to somebody. You were created for God's pleasure.

So when you open your eyes every morning, be encouraged that you are awaking for God's good pleasure. And understand that His world is crammed with solutions. Everything created is a solution...to somebody, somewhere, at some time. This means you are a solution to someone. Somebody needs you. Somebody wants you. You are necessary to somebody, somewhere...today.

Read these powerful words. They are also for you:

> *Then the word of the Lord came unto me, saying, before I formed thee in the belly I knew thee; and before thou camest forth out of the womb I sanctified thee, and I ordained thee a prophet unto the nations.*
>
> Jeremiah 1:4,5

*Like Jeremiah, you were created for a specific and very special purpose...to solve a specific problem on earth. This is your Assignment. Are you ready to discover it? Are you ready to be somebody's reward?*

# FACT 2

## You Are a Reward to Someone

### SOMEBODY NEEDS YOU

Israel needed a leader. So Moses was their reward.

David was needed by the Israelites to defeat Goliath. So he was their reward. David was a reward to King Saul as well, when he defeated Goliath and routed the Philistines.

Naomi needed a caretaker. So Ruth was her reward. In fact, Ruth was so loyal to Naomi that her devotion was recorded in the Scriptures for people to read throughout many generations.

The Jews would have been destroyed except for Esther. So Esther was their answer, their solution — their reward.

Pharaoh desperately needed someone to interpret his dream. So Joseph was his reward, and subsequently to the people of Egypt.

Famine would have destroyed the Egyptians. So Joseph was their reward because he interpreted the message from God through the dream of Pharaoh.

You see, everything God created is a reward to somebody.

Think about this. It is very important that you grasp your significance and value.

Your patience is a reward for somebody who others would not

God planned you, and nobody else can be like you.

tolerate. Your words will motivate someone incapable of seeing what you see. It may be the mental, emotional, or spiritual qualities God has developed within you, BUT SOMEBODY DESPERATELY NEEDS YOU TODAY.

God planned you, and nobody else can be like you. Nobody else can do what you do. You are unlike anyone else on earth. Grasp and embrace this. God is not a duplicator. He is a Creator. You alone are absolutely perfect and genetically accurate for solving a specific problem for somebody on earth today.

Someone needs exactly what you have been given by God. Someone is hungry and thirsty for your presence. Someone will perish unless you enter his life. Someone is literally dying, emotionally, mentally, or spiritually, waiting for you to come to his rescue. Someone has been lying awake at night praying that God would send you his way.

## YOU ARE SOMEONE'S REWARD

Now, it is important that you recognize that some people do not really need you. You are not their answer. You are not their solution. So do not take offense at this. God has someone else planned for them.

You are not needed everywhere. You are only needed at a specific place at a specific time for a specific person.

20

The person or people God sends you to will qualify for your entrance into their life. They may not initially see you as being their reward, but really, you are. You are exactly what God has ordered for their life.

Meditate on this truth. Taste it. Feel it.

### 3 IMPORTANT KEYS TO OBTAINING "YOUR" REWARD:

1. God has qualified you to be a perfect solution to someone.

2. However, it is the responsibility of others to discern your Assignment to them. Thousands who followed Jesus were sick and blind. But only one that we know of in Scripture cried out, saying, "Jesus, thou son of David, have mercy on me!" (See Mark 10:47.)

   Even Pharaoh of Egypt, an unbeliever, discerned that Joseph was the answer to his dilemma and dream. And though the Pharisees did not discern that Jesus was assigned to them, the tax collector Zacchaeus did, and the relationship was born.

3. So when you discover to whom you have been assigned, you will experience great peace, fulfillment, and provision for your own life.

   But it is you who must determine and know well the anointing and calling of your own life. So stand strong, stay linked to the Holy Spirit in total dependency, and God will direct you.

   Look for opportunities to heal, strengthen, and bless others. Do good every time it is possible to do so:

   *Withhold not good from them to whom it is due, when it is in the power of thine hand to do it.*

   Proverbs 3:27

***You are truly a gift and reward to whom you are assigned.***

**FACT**

**3**

## Your Assignment Is Not Your Decision — It Is Your Discovery

### SEEK AND YOU WILL FIND

Your Assignment is awaiting your discovery from the Holy Spirit and in the pages of Scripture. Here are some Assignment clues you need to know.

God has specifically prepared events and situations for those who love Him:

> *...Eye hath not seen, nor ear heard, neither have entered into the heart of man, the things which God hath prepared for them that love him.*
> 1 Corinthians 2:9

You will only discern or discover those things and events connected to your Assignment by the Holy Spirit:

> *But God hath revealed them unto us by his Spirit: for the Spirit searcheth all things, yea, the deep things of God.*
> 1 Corinthians 2:10

You must have the mind of Christ to discern your Assignment:

*For who hath known the mind of the Lord, that he may instruct him? But we have the mind of Christ.*

1 Corinthians 2:16

You are sent by God into this generation.

*Ask, and it shall be given you; seek, and ye shall find; knock, and it shall be opened unto you.*

Matthew 7:7

Your gifts and skills were given to you by the Holy Spirit:

*Now there are diversities of gifts, but the same Spirit.... But all these worketh that one and the selfsame Spirit, dividing to every man severally as he will.*

1 Corinthians 12:4,11

Your gifts and skills are different from others around you:

*Having then gifts differing according to the grace that is given to us, whether prophecy, let us prophesy according to the proportion of faith.*

Romans 12:6

*God also bearing them witness, both with signs and wonders, and with divers miracles, and gifts of the Holy Ghost, according to his own will.*

Hebrews 2:4

You are sent by God into this generation:

*...for thou shalt go to all that I shall send thee, and whatsoever I command thee thou shalt speak.*

Jeremiah 1:7

Your agenda has been predestined in the mind of God:

*See, I have this day set thee over the nations and over the kingdoms, to root out, and to pull down, and to destroy, and to throw down, to build, and to plant.*

Jeremiah 1:10

■ God not only has a plan.
■ God has a plan for your life.
■ His plan for your life will require your obedience:

*If ye be willing and obedient, ye shall eat the good of the land: but if ye refuse and rebel, ye shall be devoured with the sword: for the mouth of the Lord hath spoken it.*

Isaiah 1:19,20

His plan for your life will require a *personal* decision on your part to cooperate:

*And it shall come to pass, if thou shalt hearken diligently unto the voice of the Lord thy God, to observe and to do all his commandments which I command thee this day, that the Lord thy God will set thee on high above all nations of the earth.*

Deuteronomy 28:1

His plan guarantees His blessing when completed:

*And all these blessings shall come on thee, and overtake thee, if thou shalt hearken unto the voice of the Lord thy God. Blessed shalt thou be in the city, and blessed shalt thou be in the field.*

Deuteronomy 28:2,3

His plan gives life to you — other plans bring death:

*I call heaven and earth to record this day against you, that I have set before you life and death, blessing and cursing: therefore choose life, that both thou and thy seed may live.*

Deuteronomy 30:19

- God *decides* what you are to do.
- Your decision is to *obey*.

Predestination is the intention of God, not the decision of God:

*The Lord is not slack concerning his promise, as some men count slackness; but is longsuffering to us-ward, not willing that any should perish, but that all should come to repentance.*

2 Peter 3:9

Think for a moment. Did the automobile instruct Henry Ford and declare to him what it had decided to be? Of course not. Mr. Ford named it. Did the airplane inform the Wright brothers that it was going to fly and be called an airplane? Of course not. Orville and Wilbur Wright declared it to be so.

And we know that God does not want anyone to perish. Yet, they do. Daily. Millions have perished without Christ. So even though you were predestined (intended by God) to be saved, it remains your decision to cooperate with Him and accept Him.

- The Creator *decides*.
- The creation *discovers*.

*O Jerusalem, Jerusalem, thou that killest the prophets, and stonest them which are sent unto thee, how often would*

*I have gathered thy children together, even as a hen gathereth her chickens under her wings, and ye would not! Behold, your house is left unto you desolate.*

Matthew 23:37,38

- ■ The Creator decides what He has intended you to become. The creation merely decides the degree of obedience and cooperation to make it so.
- ■ Products do not decide.
- ■ Manufacturers decide.

*Remember, you are the product of God. And He is the only One who can reveal the Assignment He decided for you at your birth.*

**FACT 4**

# Your Assignment Will Require Your Total Focus

## The Only Reason Men Fail Is Because of Broken Focus

While traveling around the world for more than thirty years and speaking more than twelve thousand times, I have listened to the details of the personal battles and conflicts of many hurting people. And as I have listened, I have learned a very important truth: An important goal of Satan is to simply break the focus of God's people from off of their Assignments. Focus is anything that consumes your time, energy, finances, and attention. So if Satan can blur the focus of your Assignment, he can master you. And if he can master you, he can bring pain to the heart of God, who is his only true enemy.

How important is your focus?

Listen to the words of God concerning those who would tempt His people to go to another god:

> *If thy brother, the son of thy mother, or thy son, or thy daughter, or the wife of thy bosom, or thy friend, which is as thine own soul, entice thee secretly, saying, Let us go and serve other gods, which thou hast not known, thou, nor thy fathers; namely, of the gods of the people which are round about you, nigh unto thee, or far off from thee, from the one end of the earth even unto the other end of the earth; thou shalt not consent unto him, nor hearken unto him; neither shall thine eye pity him, neither shalt thou spare, neither shalt thou conceal him: but thou shalt surely kill him; thine hand shall be first upon him to put him to death, and afterwards the hand of all the people. And thou shalt stone him with stones, that he die; because he hath sought to thrust thee away from the Lord thy God, which brought thee out of the land of Egypt, from the house of bondage.*

> Deuteronomy 13:6-10

How do you destroy someone's goal? Give him another goal.

Now listen to how Jesus addressed broken focus in the New Testament:

> *And if thy right eye offend thee, pluck it out, and cast it from thee: for it is profitable for thee that one of thy members should perish, and not that thy whole body should be cast into hell. And if thy right hand offend thee, cut it off, and cast it from thee: for it is profitable for thee that one of*

*thy members should perish, and not that thy whole body should be cast into hell.*

Matthew 5:29,30

Jesus encouraged His disciples to keep their focus on the kingdom of God. He assured them that their financial provisions and everything they needed would be produced through absolute focus upon Him:

*But seek ye first the kingdom of God, and his righteousness; and all these things shall be added unto you.*

Matthew 6:33

How do you destroy someone's goal? Give him another goal. How do you destroy another's dream? You give him another dream. Why? It fragments his focus. It dilutes his energy. So to avoid this in your Assignment, here are twelve wisdom principles on FOCUS that can make a real difference in your life:

## 12 FOCUS WISDOM PRINCIPLES

1. Focus determines mastery. And anything that has the ability to keep your attention has mastered you. So any significant progress toward the completion of your Assignment will require every thought, cent, and hour of your life.

2. Your focus determines your energy. Think for a moment. Let us say you are sleepy, laid back on your pillows, and the television is on. Then suddenly, the telephone rings. Someone in your family has just had a crisis and they are being rushed to the hospital. Do you go back to sleep? Of course not. Your focus has been changed. Suddenly, you have leaped to your feet, put your clothes on, jumped in your car, and are headed to the hospital. Your new focus gave you new energy. It determined your energy.

3. What you look at the longest becomes the strongest in your life. The apostle Paul focused on his future:

> *Brethren, I count not myself to have apprehended: but this one thing I do, forgetting those things which are behind, and reaching forth unto those things which are before, I press toward the mark for the prize of the high calling of God in Christ Jesus.*
>
> Philippians 3:13,14

4. Broken focus creates insecurity and instability in everything around you:

> *A double minded man is unstable in all his ways.*
>
> James 1:8

5. Only focused faith can produce miracles from the hand of God:

> *But let him ask in faith, nothing wavering. For he that wavereth is like a wave of the sea driven with the wind and tossed. For let not that man think that he shall receive any thing of the Lord.*
>
> James 1:6,7

6. Sight affects desire. What you keep looking upon, you will eventually pursue:

> *Mine eye affecteth mine heart....*
>
> Lamentations 3:51

Joshua, the remarkable leader of the Israelites, wrote this instruction from God:

> *Only be thou strong and very courageous, that thou mayest observe to do according to all the law, which Moses my servant commanded thee: turn not from it to the right hand or to the left, that thou mayest prosper whithersoever*

*thou goest. This book of the law shall not depart out of thy mouth; but thou shalt meditate therein day and night, that thou mayest observe to do according to all that is written therein: for then thou shalt make thy way prosperous, and then thou shalt have good success.*

Joshua 1:7,8

7. Focusing on the Word of God daily is necessary to complete your Assignment properly. God instructed the people of Israel to teach, train, and mentor their children. Why? His Words. Listen to this incredible instruction:

*Therefore shall ye lay up these my words in your heart and in your soul, and bind them for a sign upon your hand, that they may be as frontlets between your eyes. And ye shall teach them your children, speaking of them when thou sittest in thine house, and when thou walkest by the way, when thou liest down, and when thou risest up. And thou shalt write them upon the door posts of thine house, and upon thy gates.*

Deuteronomy 11:18-20

8. Focusing, hearing, and speaking the Word of God continuously makes you invincible. This is one of the reasons I keep cassettes of the Word of God in every room of my home. The first thing I do daily is turn on my tape player to listen to the Scriptures being read. It washes my mind, purges my heart, and harnesses my focus:

*There shall no man be able to stand before you: for the Lord your God shall lay the fear of you and the dread of you upon all the land that ye shall tread upon, as he hath said unto you.*

Deuteronomy 11:25

9. Focus has reward:

*That your days may be multiplied, and the days of your children, in the land which the Lord sware unto your fathers to give them, as the days of heaven upon the earth. For if ye shall diligently keep all these commandments which I command you, to do them, to love the Lord your God, to walk in all his ways, and to cleave unto him; then will the Lord drive out all these nations from before you, and ye shall possess greater nations and mightier than yourselves. Every place whereon the soles of your feet shall tread shall be yours....*

Deuteronomy 11:21-24

10. What you keep seeing determines your focus:

*I will set no wicked thing before mine eyes: I hate the work of them that turn aside; it shall not cleave to me.*

Psalm 101:3

11. Your enemy is anyone who breaks your focus from a God-given Assignment:

*Do thy diligence to come shortly unto me: for Demas hath forsaken me, having loved this present world, and is departed unto Thessalonica; Crescens to Galatia, Titus unto Dalmatia.*

2 Timothy 4:9,10

12. Your friend is anyone who helps keep you focused on the instructions of God for your life:

*Having confidence in thy obedience I wrote unto thee, knowing that thou wilt also do more than I say.*

Philemon 1:21

## 6 KEYS THAT WILL HELP YOU PROTECT YOUR FOCUS

1. Recognize that broken focus will destroy your dreams.

   Distraction from your Assignment will create an unending parade of tragedies and disasters in your life.

2. Take personal responsibility.

   Be the gatekeeper of your eyes, ears, and heart. Nobody else can fully protect you. You will be protected by God, as you yield yourself to Him.

3. Control the music and teaching that enters your ears.

   What you hear determines what you feel. What you hear also determines what you fear:

   *And all Israel shall hear, and fear, and shall do no more any such wickedness as this is among you.*

   Deuteronomy 13:11

4. Keep continuous praise on your lips and music throughout your home.

   I keep music playing twenty-four hours a day on my property and in my house. The rooms throughout my home have sound, and there is music to the Holy Spirit being sung and played every minute. I have twenty-four speakers on the trees in my seven-acre yard. I am determined to protect my focus.

5. Starve wrong friendships.

Wrong friends do not feed, fuel, or fertilize the total focus of your Assignment. So let those friendships die. Samson did not have to date everyone to get his hair cut. It only required one wrong person to destroy his future.

6. Pursue and permit only those relationships that increase your focus on your Assignment.

It was late one night in southern Florida. The service had ended, and several of the ministers wanted to go to a restaurant. As we sat there, I listened to their conversation. I have two major interests in my life: learning and teaching. And both must take place continuously for me to have pleasure!

So I sat there and listened as everyone discussed ball games, politics, and tragedies. I kept listening for worthy Wisdom Keys that might be imparted, and for important questions that might be asked. But neither took place. Several times I even attempted to change the direction of the conversation, but it seemed to be ignored. The Holy Spirit was not the focus, and I was too tired to force the conversation in an appropriate direction. So I quietly stood and said, "I must leave. God bless each of you." Then I left. I wish I could have that kind of courage every year of my lifetime, every day of my life.

*Focus is the Master Key to the Golden Door of Success.*

# FACT
# 5

## Your Assignment Will Require Time

### Time Is the Currency of Earth

Your Assignment will require time — more than you realize. It will require preparation time; seasons of negotiation; seasons of insignificance; seasons of meditation; seasons of agitation. And yes, even seasons of warfare.

Just as the peso is the currency of Mexico, the dollar is the currency of the United States, and the franc is the currency of France, the currency of earth is TIME.

God uses time to achieve His own goals on earth. He uses time to develop the seeds of greatness that He plants in the soil of people.

Think about this: God did not give you friends. He gave you time, and you invested time into people and created friendships. Neither did God give you money. Again, He gave you time. And you exchanged your time for paper money from your employer.

37

Moses was trained by God for eighty years before he became a great deliverer. Jesus invested thirty years of time before He began His earthly ministry of three and one-half years.

> *To every thing there is a season, and a time to every purpose under the heaven: a time to be born, and a time to die; a time to plant, and a time to pluck up that which is planted; a time to kill, and a time to heal; a time to break down, and a time to build up; a time to weep, and a time to laugh; a time to mourn, and a time to dance; a time to cast away stones, and a time to gather stones together; a time to embrace, and a time to refrain from embracing; a time to get, and a time to lose; a time to keep, and a time to cast away; a time to rend, and a time to sew; a time to keep silence, and a time to speak; a time to love, and a time to hate; a time of war, and a time of peace... He hath made every thing beautiful in his time: also he hath set the world in their heart, so that no man can find out the work that God maketh from the beginning to the end.*
>
> Ecclesiastes 3:1-8,11

> *In a sense, you can never really see your future. Because when you arrive there, you call it "today."*

## GREATNESS WILL COST YOU THE CURRENCY OF TIME

- ■ It takes TIME to develop a strong relationship with your mentor.
- ■ It takes TIME to establish a proven reputation of integrity.

■ It takes TIME to carefully build a financial foundation for a great future.

■ It takes TIME to extract information from the crisis of a critical moment in your life.

■ It takes TIME to be restored when you have made a major mistake.

*And let us not be weary in well doing: for in due season we shall reap, if we faint not.*

Galatians 6:9

Someone has well said that it is impossible to save time and that you must simply learn to invest it wisely:

*Redeeming the time, because the days are evil.*

Ephesians 5:16

## FOCUS ON CREATING A PERFECT DAY

You see, in a sense, you can never really see your future. Because when you arrive there, you call it "today." Yesterday is over. Tomorrow is not yet here.

■ *Yesterday* is in the tomb.

■ *Tomorrow* is in the womb.

■ *Today* is really your life.

## TO HELP YOU MAKE YOUR TIME COUNT— USE THESE 9 KEYS

1. Focus on carefully planning the next 24 hours.

2. Concentrate on making each hour a productive hour.

3. Schedule an hour of movement toward wisdom (reading the Word of God).

4. Schedule another hour of movement toward the Holy Spirit and receiving counsel, prayer time in *The Secret Place* (Psalm 91:1).

5. Schedule one hour of movement toward health. Exercise daily.

6. Schedule one hour to monitor, mentor, and motivate your Love Circle. These are those you love who are linked to your Assignment.

7. Schedule an hour for restoration. (It may be a nap or simply relaxing and watching the news for a half hour. This is restoration time.)

8. Guard access to yourself. Qualify those who enter your arena of life. They must desire what you possess or must possess something you desire.

9. Unclutter your life by uncluttering your day. Eliminate the things that God did not specifically tell you to do.

When you learn to create a perfect day, you can make it happen every day of your life. And when you learn to take control of your time, the fruit of patience will become a powerful virtue in your life.

Patience is the force that makes faith productive. The patience of God has produced millions of saved lives. He was willing to patiently build a road into your life until you found Him believable and accepted His authority in your life. And He has been patiently waiting for your acceptance of His life Assignment.

■ So take the TIME to *discover* your Assignment.

■ Then *invest* the TIME necessary to do it right.

***Patience is often as powerful as faith.***

# FACT
# 6

## Your Assignment Will Require Seasons of Preparation

### You Are Not Born Qualified — So You Must Become Qualified

Once you recognize the time that your Assignment will require, get ready to prepare. Get ready for God's seasons.

Look at the life of Moses. He spent his first forty years learning the wisdom of the Egyptians:

> *And Moses was learned in all the wisdom of the Egyptians, and was mighty in words and in deeds. And when he was full forty years old, it came into his heart to visit his brethren the children of Israel.*

Acts 7:22,23

Then he spent another forty years learning the lessons of leadership and the priesthood:

*Now Moses kept the flock of Jethro his father-in-law, the priest of Midian: and he led the flock to the backside of the desert, and came to the mountain of God, even to Horeb.*

Exodus 3:1

Get ready for God's seasons.

*And when forty years were expired, there appeared to him in the wilderness of mount Sina an angel of the Lord in a flame of fire in a bush. When Moses saw it, he wondered at the sight: and as he drew near to behold it, the voice of the Lord came unto him.*

Acts 7:30,31

Moses was a protégé for eighty years. During his first forty years, he was a general in the Egyptian army. During his second forty years, he was the shepherd of hundreds of sheep.

## PREPARATION. PREPARATION. PREPARATION. LOOK AT THE LIFE OF JESUS

Jesus spent thirty years preparing for His ministry:

*But when the fulness of the time was come, God sent forth his Son, made of a woman, made under the law, to redeem them that were under the law, that we might receive the adoption of sons.*

Galatians 4:4,5

*And the Holy Ghost descended in a bodily shape like a dove upon him, and a voice came from heaven, which said, Thou art my beloved Son; in thee I am well pleased. And Jesus himself began to be about thirty years of age....*

Luke 3:22,23

These days seem so different for young ministers. The average young minister wants to prepare three and a half years for thirty years of public ministry. But Jesus did the opposite. He prepared thirty years for a public ministry of three and a half years.

## Look at the apostle Paul

He was a Pharisee, and the son of a Pharisee (Acts 23:6). He had invested years of preparation for the intelligentsia of his generation:

> *If any other man thinketh that he hath whereof he might trust in the flesh, I more: circumcised the eighth day, of the stock of Israel, of the tribe of Benjamin, an Hebrew of the Hebrews; as touching the law, a Pharisee; concerning zeal, persecuting the church; touching the righteousness which is of the law, blameless.*
>
> Philippians 3:4-6

Yet, that was not enough preparation:

> *But what things were gain to me, those I counted loss for Christ.*
>
> Philippians 3:7

God had another three-year school for him:

> *Neither went I up to Jerusalem to them which were apostles before me; but I went into Arabia, and returned again unto Damascus. Then after three years I went up to Jerusalem to see Peter, and abode with him fifteen days.*
>
> Galatians 1:17,18

And Paul mentored others concerning fourteen seasons of life in the ministry —

1. Seasons of affliction —

> *...but be thou partaker of the afflictions of the gospel according to the power of God....*
>
> 2 Timothy 1:8

> *It is good for me that I have been afflicted; that I might learn thy statutes.*
>
> Psalm 119:71

2. Seasons of solitude —

> *Greatly desiring to see thee, being mindful of thy tears, that I may be filled with joy.*
>
> 2 Timothy 1:4

3. Seasons of warfare —

> *Thou therefore endure hardness, as a good soldier of Jesus Christ. No man that warreth entangleth himself with the affairs of this life; that he may please him who hath chosen him to be a soldier.*
>
> 2 Timothy 2:3,4

4. Seasons of suffering —

> *If we suffer, we shall also reign with him: if we deny him, he also will deny us.*
>
> 2 Timothy 2:12

5. Seasons of learning —

> *Study to shew thyself approved unto God, a workman that needeth not to be ashamed, rightly dividing the word of truth.*
>
> 2 Timothy 2:15

6. Seasons of carnal desires —

*Flee also youthful lusts: but follow righteousness, faith, charity, peace, with them that call on the Lord out of a pure heart.*

2 Timothy 2:22

7. Seasons of contention —

*But foolish and unlearned questions avoid, knowing that they do gender strifes. And the servant of the Lord must not strive; but be gentle unto all men, apt to teach, patient.*

2 Timothy 2:23,24

8. Seasons of persecution —

*Persecutions, afflictions, which came unto me...what persecutions I endured: but out of them all the Lord delivered me. Yea, and all that will live godly in Christ Jesus shall suffer persecution.*

2 Timothy 3:11,12

9. Seasons of proving —

*But watch thou in all things, endure afflictions, do the work of an evangelist, make full proof of thy ministry.*

2 Timothy 4:5

10. Seasons of disloyalty —

*For Demas hath forsaken me, having loved this present world, and is departed unto Thessalonica....*

2 Timothy 4:10

11. Seasons of injustice —

*Alexander the coppersmith did me much evil: the Lord reward him according to his works.*

2 Timothy 4:14

12. Seasons of isolation —

> *At my first answer no man stood with me, but all men forsook me: I pray God that it may not be laid to their charge.*
>
> 2 Timothy 4:16

13. Seasons of supernatural intervention —

> *Notwithstanding the Lord stood with me, and strengthened me; that by me the preaching might be fully known, and that all the Gentiles might hear....*
>
> 2 Timothy 4:17

14. Seasons of deliverance —

> *...I was delivered out of the mouth of the lion. And the Lord shall deliver me from every evil work, and will preserve me unto his heavenly kingdom: to whom be glory for ever and ever. Amen.*
>
> 2 Timothy 4:17,18

As you read about the apostle Paul's life in the book of Acts and in his church epistles, it is powerfully evident that in every one of his seasons, he walked in total VICTORY. So you can expect to walk in total victory too — regardless of the season.

> *Nay, in all these things we are more than conquerors through him that loved us.*
>
> Romans 8:37

Did you ever see the movie, "The Karate Kid"? It contains some powerful lessons. In the story, the young boy desperately wanted to learn the art of fighting. His old mentor wanted to teach him how to fight as well. But instead of suiting up and heading for the ring, he waited, and handed the young man a paint brush with instructions to paint his fence. The young man was disheartened, but he followed his mentor's instructions.

Discouraged, disillusioned, and very disappointed, the kid could not see any relationship between painting a fence and fighting in the ring. Then when he was finished, his mentor gave him the assignment of washing and waxing his car. As he moved his hands in a circular motion over the car, he felt very demoralized and thought, *How will this help me in my future? How will this help me achieve my desire to be a great fighter?*

But as the kid worked in confusion and despair, the older and much wiser mentor knew that each motion of his student's hands would develop the hands of a fighter. The young man did not discern it until much later. And when he did — it all made sense.

Like the Karate Kid, I can look back on many seasons of my fifty years of life in which I felt ignorant and unaware of the purpose of that specific season. In many of them, I would wonder, "How could God get any glory out of this situation?" But now I can see how He divinely intervened. He taught me so much.

Never forget that your heavenly Father knows what He is doing with your life:

> *But he knoweth the way that I take: when he hath tried me, I shall come forth as gold.*
>
> Job 23:10

Sometimes you will not discern His presence:

> *Behold, I go forward, but he is not there; and backward, but I cannot perceive him: on the left hand, where he doth work, but I cannot behold him; he hideth himself on the right hand, that I cannot see him.*
>
> Job 23:8,9

Yes, you will even experience seasons of chastening:

*For whom the Lord loveth he chasteneth, and scourgeth every son whom he receiveth... Now no chastening for the present seemeth to be joyous, but grievous: nevertheless afterward it yieldeth the peaceable fruit of righteousness unto them which are exercised thereby.*

Hebrews 12:6,11

So fully embrace and have expectation in the present season God has scheduled for your life. Extract every possible benefit:

*Wherefore lift up the hands which hang down, and the feeble knees.*

Hebrews 12:12

You will survive the fires of the furnace:

*Though I walk in the midst of trouble, thou wilt revive me: thou shalt stretch forth thine hand against the wrath of mine enemies, and thy right hand shall save me.*

Psalm 138:7

You are being perfected for your Assignment:

*The Lord will perfect that which concerneth me.*

Psalm 138:8

*Your success is inevitable!*

# FACT 7

## WHAT YOU LOVE IS A CLUE TO THE GIFTS, SKILLS, AND WISDOM YOU POSSESS

### YOU ARE UNIQUE

You possess certain qualities, specific gifts and worthy traits that make you unique. They distinguish you from the herd.

So what is it that makes you unique? What do you love to talk about most? What subjects get you the most excited? I asked my staff recently, "If every human on earth was paid $10 an hour for work, regardless of the type of job, what would you do? For example, if you chose to be the janitor of a building, you would receive $10 an hour for it. And if you decided that you wanted to be a heart surgeon, you would still receive $10 an hour. What would you love to do if money was no longer a factor in it?" Then I said, "When you find that out: YOU HAVE FOUND YOUR ASSIGNMENT."

### LOVE BIRTHS WISDOM

Let me explain.

When you have a love for children, a special wisdom begins to grow and develop in you toward children. You begin to understand their fears, tears, and desires.

When you have a love for animals, you develop an intuition, a special wisdom for their behavior and conduct. You can sense what they are feeling.

> *Find what you truly and continuously love, then build your daily agenda around it.*

In the same way, when you need wisdom in your marriage, a love for your mate must be birthed first. So wisdom is the product of love. Love births persistence. When you love something, you give birth to extraordinary tenacity, determination, and persistence.

Recently, I read a powerful story about a runner. In his youth, he had a terrible disease. Doctors insisted he would never be able to even walk again. But something powerful was within him. He loved running.

His love for running birthed determination and he ended up winning a gold medal in the Olympics.

Love is stronger than sickness. It is stronger than disease. It is stronger than poverty.

So find what you truly and continuously love, then build your daily agenda around it.

Moses loved people. When he saw an Egyptian beating a fellow Israelite, he moved quickly. Then in his passion for justice, he killed the Egyptian. That was unfortunate. It postponed his Assignment. But Moses' love for his people was a clue to his mantle as a deliverer. He was attentive to the cries. He cared. His compassion ran deep. And because he had a love for people, he was able to lead people. They followed him. Yes, they complained, whined, and griped — but they had found their leader.

Abraham loved peace. He despised conflict. So when God decided to destroy Sodom and Gomorrah, Abraham became an intercessor and mediator for his nephew Lot, who lived in the wicked city. Then when Sodom and Gomorrah were destroyed, Lot and his daughters were brought out safely. They were rescued because Abraham contained something very precious: a love for peace. And God rewarded it. Abraham's love for peace birthed the wisdom necessary to achieve it.

Recently, a close friend of mine came to our ministry and gave a special teaching. He gave us a personality profile to help us discover the greatest gifts within us. He showed us how to examine the lives of Bible characters and showed us how we relate to them. This is one of the most important things you can do. You must find what you really care about and develop your life around it. The experience was a blessing.

It is wise to alter and change the flaws within us. But it is even wiser to acknowledge and embrace the center of God's calling to permit the true you to become strong.

I have often heard people insistently tell a shy person, "You must talk more!" Then that same person will turn to someone talking a lot and say, "Be quiet! Just sit and listen!" We also instruct youth to "get more serious about life" before we instruct the elderly to "be less serious and lighten up!"

So understand the importance of your uniqueness. Then do not move away from the essence of what God made you. Discern your gifts. Name your calling. Build your daily agenda around it. Whatever you are gifted to do is what you should be doing.

*What you truly love the most is a clue to a marvelous gift and quality inside of you.*

# FACT
# 8

## WHAT GRIEVES YOU IS
## A CLUE TO SOMETHING YOU
## ARE ASSIGNED TO HEAL

### TEARS TALK

What you cry about is a clue to something you were created and ordained by God to heal. Compassion is a signpost.

What grieves you? Battered wives? Abused and molested children? Ignorance? Disease? Poverty? Pornography? Homosexuality? Abortion? Name it. Be honest with yourself. Caring qualifies you as an instrument of healing.

What makes you cry is a clue to a problem God has anointed you to conquer, change, and heal. Look at Nehemiah. His heart was broken about the walls of Jerusalem which were broken down. He could not sleep at night. He could not rest. He wept long hours.

Everything within Nehemiah was stirred to fast and pray, to obtain the king's letters, and to connect with the governors and other officials who could help complete his mission of rebuilding

Jerusalem's walls. And he was more than willing to change his personal life to get the job done.

Also look at Ezra. His heart was broken over the temple in Jerusalem. He could not rest. He wept and sobbed. He read Scriptures to the people. He knew that the presence of God was the only remedy for wounded people. He recognized that places mattered, and that God would honor and reward those who sanctified a worship center in the city. Those feelings were signposts to Ezra's Assignment.

> *What you cry about is a clue to something you were created and ordained by God to heal.*

There is an insanity in our society today. Observe how the liquor industry has made sure their advertisements get pasted on every billboard in our sporting stadiums. And look at how every newspaper is filled with liquor advertisements. Yet, alcohol has murdered and destroyed more people on our streets and highways than those lost in the entire Vietnam war.

Someone has said that we have lost more of our children to death through alcoholism than every death combined in every major war. Yet, everyone screams about the horrors of war while sipping their alcohol at a cocktail table.

Someday, God is going to raise up another champion like Billy Sunday. Someone who is tired of crying over children's brains splattered on a highway. Someone who will be so grieved over senseless deaths that their Assignment, like Billy Sunday's, will be very clear. Then his Assignment will become an obsession like Ezra's and Nehemiah's, and he will rise up to launch a war...a holy war that will salvage the lives of thousands, and heal the broken in this generation.

Have you wept long hours over financial bankruptcy and debt? Think of the many families in America who lack finances because of a father's drinking habit. Think of the children who cannot be put through school because money is wasted on alcohol. Do you weep when you see homeless children? Tears are clues to where God will use you the most.

Oh, there are many things that should set us on fire. But what grieves you? What saddens you? What moves you to tears? Pay attention to it. Tears are clues to the nature of your Assignment.

*Where you hurt the most is a clue to what you may heal the best.*

# FACT 9

## WHAT YOU HATE IS A CLUE TO SOMETHING YOU ARE ASSIGNED TO CORRECT

### ANGER IS ENERGY, POWER, AND ABILITY

However, because of anger's power potential, it requires proper focus. Have you ever wondered why others were not angry about situations that infuriated you? Of course you have. This is a clue to your Assignment.

Again, Moses is a good example. He hated slavery. When he saw an Egyptian beating an Israelite, fury arose. Why? Because he was called to be a deliverer.

### REMEMBER THESE 3 WISDOM KEYS

1. You cannot correct what you are unwilling to confront.

2. What you permit will always continue.

3. Behavior permitted is behavior perpetuated.

I have a special love for wisdom. And I have a hatred of ignorance. In my own life I have attended seminars where Scriptures were misquoted, truth was distorted, and error was dominant. It was almost impossible for me to sit and permit it.

You cannot really change or correct something unless you have a God-given hatred for it, whether it is sickness, injustice, racial prejudice, poverty, divorce, or abortion.

*Focused fury is often the key to miraculous change.*

Many things are wrong in this country. But they will never be changed until someone is angry enough about it to step forward and take charge.

For instance, abortion has subtly become accepted, even though it is a truly devastating blight on the moral landscape of this country. It appears that no true and articulate spokesperson has yet emerged who is capable of turning the tide, though I do thank God for those who are making significant efforts to do so!

## THE PERSUADED ARE PERSUASIVE

I have asked God often to give us someone with a burning desire who can successfully plead the case of the unborn child. I have asked God to provide a militant, intellectual, passionate zealot who will link the Word of God with the gift of life in my generation — someone passionate and on fire.

## THAT SOMEONE COULD BE YOU

I am not talking about the issue of bombing abortion clinics or murdering others who kill unborn children.

I am speaking of an anointing, a mantle, a calling — someone who will rise up to complete their Assignment in this generation to challenge, correct, and conquer the seeds of rebellion that have grown up around us.

Your anger is important. Very important. So do not ignore it. Satan dreads your fury. An angry man is an awakened man who can change the minds of others.

***Focused fury is often the key to miraculous change.***

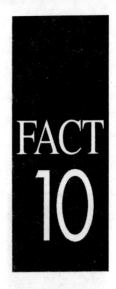

# FACT 10

## YOUR ASSIGNMENT
## IS GEOGRAPHICAL

### PLACES MATTER

Some time ago, at lunch, a minister friend shared an interesting story with me. "Mike," he said, "when I lived one hundred miles away from Dallas, I had fair success...nothing extraordinary. But the moment I moved to Dallas, our church here absolutely exploded in attendance. I knew immediately that I was in the right place at the right time."

God made places before He made people. Therefore, where you are is as important as what you are.

### WHERE YOU ARE DETERMINES
### WHAT GROWS WITHIN YOU

Your weaknesses and your strengths require a climate. Jesus knew geography mattered: "And he must needs go through Samaria" (John 4:4). He could have added, "Because there is a woman there who needs Me who will reach the entire city!"

Read the Samaritan woman's account in John 4:1-42 carefully and you will learn that Jesus knew this one person was in need of Him that very day.

When Moses was wandering around Mt. Seir, God spoke to him and said, "Ye have compassed this mountain long enough: turn you northward" (Deuteronomy 2:3).

> *Where you are is as important as what you are.*

Jonah was instructed to go to Nineveh. But he rebelled, and the whole world has since read his diary of attending "Whale University"!

Abraham was instructed by God to leave his father's house in Ur of the Chaldees to set out for a new land.

Ruth left Moab and followed her mother-in-law Naomi back to Bethlehem where she met Boaz!

Esther was raised by Mordecai. But when God was ready to bless her, He moved her into the palace.

Five hundred were instructed by Jesus to go to the upper room. Only 120 obeyed, and it was only that 120 who received the promised blessing.

You cannot work on the wrong job, for the wrong boss, doing the wrong things for forty hours a week and wonder why two hours a week in church does not change your life! So I hope you can now see how geography plays a major part in every success story.

## GOD WILL NOT BLESS YOU JUST ANYWHERE YOU GO

He will bless you, however, if you are willing to go anywhere in order to obey and please Him. Yes, it is true: Where you are determines what grows within you, weeds or flowers, strengths or weaknesses.

Have you ever noticed when you are in the presence of certain friends that you laugh at different kinds of jokes? Have you ever noticed how the topic of your conversation often changes, depending on the person you are around?

## 2 GEOGRAPHY KEYS

### 1. Where you are determines who sees you.

Those who see you determine the favor that comes toward you. And nobody receives favor unless he is SEEN. Joseph did not get promoted until Pharaoh saw him. Ruth did not receive favor until Boaz saw her. The blind man received no instructions for healing until Jesus saw him. The daughter of Pharaoh did not show favor to the little baby Moses in the basket until she saw him.

### 2. Geography matters.

Geography controls the flow of favor in your life. And never forget — one day of favor is worth a thousand days of labor. So go where you are celebrated instead of where you are tolerated. Seek to be where God wants you, daily, hourly, weekly. Become more conscious of where you are, where you work, and for whom you work. It is so sad that some people simply take a newspaper and start calling places to look for a job instead of sitting in the presence of God and asking Him, "To whom have I been sent today?"

Somebody is supposed to succeed because of you. Who is it? To whom have you been sent? You see, when you are with the right people, the best comes out of you, and the worst part of you will die.

*Your success is always linked to a place: the place of your Assignment.*

## GOD CAN FORGIVE ANY SIN OR MISTAKE YOU HAVE MADE IN PURSUIT OF YOUR ASSIGNMENT

### FAILURE OCCURS

God is not surprised by it. He knows that men fall, and He knows how to turn it for good:

> *The steps of a good man are ordered by the Lord: and he delighteth in his way. Though he fall, he shall not be utterly cast down: for the Lord upholdeth him with his hand.*
>
> Psalm 37:23,24

Good men may even sometimes fall more than once:

> *For a just man falleth seven times, and riseth up again....*
>
> Proverbs 24:16

Even those who walked with Jesus daily, failed.

Jesus predicted it. Read what He said to Peter: "Verily, verily, I say unto thee, The cock shall not crow, till thou hast denied me thrice" (John 13:38). Then, just as Jesus said, it happened: "Peter then denied again: and immediately the cock crew" (John 18:27).

But Jesus did not condemn, criticize, or destroy Peter. He simply forgave him. Then, He turned Peter into one of the most magnificent and powerful soulwinners recorded in the New Testament:

*Even those who walked with Jesus daily, failed.*

> *Then Peter said unto them, Repent, and be baptized every one of you in the name of Jesus Christ for the remission of sins...*
>
> *Then they that gladly received his word were baptized: and the same day there were added unto them about three thousand souls.*
>
> Acts 2:38,41

And Peter went on to write two of the most powerful books of the New Testament! (See 1 and 2 Peter.)

First, Jesus birthed hope in Peter by showing him a photograph of his future victories:

> *And I say also unto thee, That thou art Peter, and upon this rock I will build my church; and the gates of hell shall not prevail against it.*
>
> Matthew 16:18

Then, Jesus sowed into his life the very keys of the kingdom:

> *And I will give unto thee the keys of the kingdom of heaven: and whatsoever thou shalt bind on earth shall be bound in heaven: and whatsoever thou shalt loose on earth shall be loosed in heaven.*
>
> Matthew 16:19

Then, Jesus alerted Peter to his enemy, Satan, to increase his caution and guardedness:

> *And the Lord said, Simon, Simon, behold, Satan hath desired to have you, that he may sift you as wheat.*
>
> Luke 22:31

Then, Jesus promised to be Peter's personal intercessor, to pray for him:

> *But I have prayed for thee, that thy faith fail not....*
>
> Luke 22:32

Then finally, Jesus gave Peter an Assignment that showed His personal confidence in believing Peter could complete it:

> *...and when thou art converted, strengthen thy brethren.*
>
> Luke 22:32

One of the saddest and most heartbreaking chapters in the entire Bible is 2 Samuel 11. David, one of the greatest champions of the faith, fell into immorality. First he committed the sin of adultery with Bathsheba. But he went one step further: he decided to have her husband murdered in battle. Then, Nathan, the man of God showed up at David's house.

## PENALTIES ALWAYS OCCUR

If God did not penalize rebellion, it would be impossible to have faith in the fact that He rewards obedience. And judgment did come. David's child died. Then his son raped his daughter, and another son murdered one of his own sons.

But David had an ability that surpassed his skill on the harp. It surpassed his ability as a warrior on the battlefield, and it surpassed his skills of supervising the entire kingdom.

David had the ability to repent:

> *And David said unto Nathan, I have sinned against the Lord. And Nathan said unto David, The Lord also hath put away thy sin; thou shalt not die.*

> 2 Samuel 12:13

## HAVE YOU FAILED?

Like David, has your heart been broken over your mistake? If it has, don't worry. A royal invitation has been sent to your house today:

> *Come now, and let us reason together, saith the Lord: though your sins be as scarlet, they shall be as white as snow; though they be red like crimson, they shall be as wool.*

> Isaiah 1:18

Samson is also a familiar story of failure, but many do not remember his recovery. Samson's story really involved many miracles. An angel of the Lord appeared to his mother and predicted his birth. Then she was instructed to discipline his life carefully because God had selected him to be a deliverer for Israel (Judges 13:2-5).

God blessed Samson, and the Spirit of the Lord came upon him, allowing him many supernatural experiences through his miraculous strength (Judges 14:6,19).

Enemies targeted Samson's life. They ambushed him. They carefully planned his downfall and finally found his weakness: a woman, Delilah. She was sensuous and very manipulative. She was a pawn in the hand of his enemies. She was tenacious and persistent every single day.

Delilah wanted Samson to empty his heart and tell her the deepest secret of his life:

*And it came to pass, when she pressed him daily with her words, and urged him, so that his soul was vexed unto death; that he told her all his heart, and said unto her, There hath not come a razor upon mine head; for I have been a Nazarite unto God from my mother's womb: if I be shaven, then my strength will go from me, and I shall become weak, and be like any other man.*

Judges 16:16,17

Samson failed in a tragic and horrifying way:

*...the Philistines took him, and put out his eyes, and brought him down to Gaza, and bound him with fetters of brass; and he did grind in the prison house.*

Judges 16:21

But Samson's seasons began to change:

*Howbeit the hair of his head began to grow again after he was shaven.*

Judges 16:22

When they brought him in to make sport of him in the big auditorium, Samson remembered yesterday.

- He *remembered* the presence of God.
- He *recalled* his anointing and electrifying victories. Somehow, he knew the heart of God.
- He *reached* again.

Oh, it is a fantastic day in your life when you make the decision to reach back for restoration. God has been waiting for you. Like the father of the prodigal son, He will run to meet you at the gate! Oh yes, He will!

> *And Samson called unto the Lord, and said, O Lord God, remember me, I pray thee, and strengthen me, I pray thee, only this once, O God, that I may be at once avenged of the Philistines for my two eyes. And Samson said, Let me die with the Philistines. And he bowed himself with all his might; and the house fell upon the lords, and upon all the people that were therein. So the dead which he slew at his death were more than they which he slew in his life.*
>
> Judges 16:28,30

This is not the end of Samson's story. He was mentioned hundreds of years later when God unfolded the heroes of faith in Hebrews 11. He is mentioned in the same chapter with Abraham, Isaac, Jacob, Joseph, Moses, and the prophet Samuel:

> *And what shall I more say? for the time would fail me to tell of Gedeon, and of Barak, and of Samson, and of Jephthae; of David also, and Samuel, and of the prophets: who through faith subdued kingdoms, wrought righteousness, obtained promises, stopped the mouths of lions, Quenched the violence of fire, escaped the edge of the sword, out of weakness were made strong, waxed valiant in fight, turned to flight the armies of the aliens.*
>
> Hebrews 11:32-34

## GOD DID IT FOR SAMSON AND HE CAN DO IT FOR YOU

In heaven, the sins of David and Bathsheba are never mentioned. The shame of Samson and Delilah is never discussed. You see, yesterday is over. It is ended:

*Remember ye not the former things, neither consider the things of old. Behold, I will do a new thing; now it shall spring forth; shall ye not know it? I will even make a way in the wilderness, and rivers in the desert.*

Isaiah 43:18,19

■ Your responsibility is to *reach*.
■ God's responsibility is to *respond*.

*For as the heaven is high above the earth, so great is his mercy toward them that fear him. As far as the east is from the west, so far hath he removed our transgressions from us. Like as a father pitieth his children, so the Lord pitieth them that fear him. For he knoweth our frame; he remembereth that we are dust...But the mercy of the Lord is from everlasting to everlasting upon them that fear him, and his righteousness unto children's children.*

Psalm 103:11-14,17

*You must focus again on your Assignment. Your best days are just ahead.*

# FACT
# 12

## IF YOU REBEL AGAINST YOUR ASSIGNMENT, GOD MAY PERMIT PAINFUL EXPERIENCES TO CORRECT YOU

### GOD WILL NOT BE IGNORED

God can create painful experiences...unforgettable experiences.

Jonah is a perfect example. He rebelled against God's instructions to "Arise, go to Nineveh, that great city, and cry against it; for their wickedness is come up before me" (Jonah 1:2). But instead:

> ...Jonah rose up to flee unto Tarshish from the presence of the Lord, and went down to Joppa; and he found a ship going to Tarshish: so he paid the fare thereof, and went down into it, to go with them unto Tarshish from the presence of the Lord. But the Lord sent out a great wind into the sea, and there was a mighty tempest in the sea, so that the ship was like to be broken.
>
> Jonah 1:3,4

73

Jonah had to endure three miserable days and nights in the belly of the fish before he came to his senses and accepted his Assignment to evangelize Nineveh.

## So NEVER MISJUDGE GOD

*...the waves of yesterday's disobedience will splash on the shores of today for a season.*

Never think that God will ignore tiny acts of defiance. Discipline comes. Reaction comes.

Look at the life of Joshua. He had specific instructions from God regarding the battle of Jericho. But when Achan rebelled and kept some of the spoils of war, they lost their first battle after Jericho, at Ai. In a single day, their reputation was stained, and Joshua's men lost total confidence. Why? They had ignored the command of God. Consequently, the entire nation suffered defeat until their obedience became their priority again. (See Joshua 7 and 8.)

## ONE PERSON'S DISOBEDIENCE CAN CREATE CORPORATE JUDGMENT

Few have grasped this truth. But it is possible that when one person is out of the will of God, everyone around that person must pay the price for it.

Years ago, a well-known leader made the statement that when finances became difficult for his ministry, he would go to prayer. Then one day God told him to quit praying and said, "Someone is on your staff that has no business here. That is the reason I have closed the finances off." So he fired that particular staff member, and the ministry finances began to flow again. I said it earlier, and it should be said on every page of this book, "When you get the wrong people out of your life, the wrong things stop happening."

Remember...the waves of yesterday's disobedience will splash on the shores of today for a season. So if you are walking in contradiction to God's laws, expect painful experiences on the road ahead.

## PAIN IS CORRECTIVE

It happens often in the Potter's House (see Jeremiah 18:1-4), where our Father is remolding common clay vessels for uncommon exploits.

> *It is good for me that I have been afflicted; that I might learn thy statutes.*
>
> Psalm 119:71

## FIVE REWARDS OF PAIN

1. Pain forces you to *look*...to the Word of God for answers.
2. Pain forces you to *lean*...on the arm of God instead of men.
3. Pain forces you to *learn*...where you went astray.
4. Pain forces you to *long*...for His presence and healing.
5. Pain forces you to *listen*...for changes in God's instructions.

**So do not misunderstand the hurting seasons. They birth the healing process.**

## FACT
## 13

# Your Assignment
# Will Require Miracles

## Your Assignment Will Require the Supernatural Interventions of God

Jesus said:

*" ... for without me ye can do nothing."*

John 15:5

Your Assignment will require miracles. Miracles require God. And God requires your obedience.

When Joshua and the Israelites approached Jericho, it took a miracle to bring the walls down.

When Gideon and his three hundred men took on the huge army of the Midianites, victory required an absolute miracle.

When Naaman dipped in the Jordan River to receive healing of his leprosy, it took a miracle for the healing to occur.

When the wine ran out at the marriage in Cana, it took a miracle of Jesus for the water in the water pots to be turned into wine.

When the widow of Zarephath was preparing to eat her last meal, it required a miracle for it to be multiplied. So she gave it to Elijah, and the seed she planted was multiplied. As a result, it fed Elijah and her household for the rest of the famine season.

When the armies of Pharaoh pursued the Israelites, they were drowned in the Red Sea. This required a miracle.

> *Your Assignment will always be big enough to require a miracle.*

You will require a miracle too. So read the following truths carefully to get into God's miracle flow.

### 8 MIRACLE TRUTHS THAT WILL HELP YOU UNDERSTAND THE LEADING OF GOD

1. God will never give you an Assignment that does not require His participation.

So you will always need the continuous, obvious, and necessary hand of God. You will not be able to accomplish your Assignment alone. Your Assignment will always be big enough to require a miracle.

- ■ You are wanting a *miracle*.
- ■ God is wanting a *relationship*.

2. God makes miracles necessary so you will be motivated to pursue Him and His involvement in your life.

3. Again, God will never involve Himself in a dream that you can achieve alone.

4. Every single act of God is designed to increase your dependence upon Him and your addiction to His presence:

*...he humbled thee, and suffered thee to hunger, and fed thee with manna, which thou knewest not, neither did thy*

*fathers know; that he might make thee know that man doth not live by bread only, but by every word that proceedeth out of the mouth of the Lord doth man live.*

Deuteronomy 8:3

5. Your Father refuses to be forgotten and ignored:

*Beware that thou forget not the Lord thy God, in not keeping his commandments, and his judgments, and his statutes, which I command thee this day.*

Deuteronomy 8:11

6. Your Father permits crisis to inspire memory:

*But thou shalt remember the Lord thy God: for it is he that giveth thee power to get wealth, that he may establish his covenant which he sware unto thy fathers, as it is this day.*

Deuteronomy 8:18

7. Jesus loved performing miracles:

*How God anointed Jesus of Nazareth with the Holy Ghost and with power: who went about doing good, and healing all that were oppressed of the devil; for God was with him.*

Acts 10:38

8. When Jesus spoke, each word was an invitation to a miracle. The uncertain are invited to a miracle. The poor are invited to a miracle:

*Give, and it shall be given unto you; good measure, pressed down, and shaken together, and running over, shall men give into your bosom. For with the same measure that ye mete withal it shall be measured to you again.*

Luke 6:38

Peter discovered that Jesus loved performing miracles when He invited him to walk on the water:

*And Peter answered him and said, Lord, if it be thou, bid me come unto thee on the water. And he said, Come. And when Peter was come down out of the ship, he walked on the water, to go to Jesus.*

Matthew 14:28,29

The sick are invited to a miracle. The man who had an infirmity for thirty-eight years was invited to a miracle:

*When Jesus saw him lie, and knew that he had been now a long time in that case, he saith unto him, Wilt thou be made whole?*

John 5:6

## 12 KEYS TO HELP YOU UNLOCK GOD'S FLOW OF MIRACLES INTO YOUR LIFE ASSIGNMENT

1. Recognize that any Assignment from God will require the miracles of God. You will not succeed alone.

2. Expect miracles in your life daily:

   *...for he that cometh to God must believe that he is, and that he is a rewarder of them that diligently seek him.*

   Hebrews 11:6

3. Remember, miracles will require a continuous flow of your faith:

   *But without faith it is impossible to please him....*

   Hebrews 11:6

4. Feed your faith confidence in God. Faith enters your heart when you read and hear the words of God spoken:

> *So then faith cometh by hearing, and hearing by the word of God.*
>
> Romans 10:17

5. Understand that the logic of your mind, and the faith of your heart, will collide. They will wage war with each other throughout your Assignment:

> *For the flesh lusteth against the Spirit, and the Spirit against the flesh: and these are contrary the one to the other: so that ye cannot do the things that ye would...But the fruit of the Spirit is...faith....*
>
> Galatians 5:17,22

6. Logic produces order, but faith produces miracles. Therefore, God will never consult your logic to determine your future. He permits your faith to determine the levels of your promotions and victories.

7. Logic is the wonderful and valuable gift He gives you to create order in your dealings with people.

8. Faith is the wonderful and valuable gift He gives you to create miracles — through the Father.

9. Your Assignment will require miracle relationships with mentors, protégés, friends, and connections. For example, Joseph would never have gotten to the palace without his miracle relationship with the butler. The relationship was a divine connection.

10. Your Assignment may require supernatural financial provision. For example, Peter experienced the miracle of finding the coin in the mouth of a fish to pay taxes. Financial miracles are normal in the lives of those who obey God.

11. Your Assignment will require the miracle of wisdom. Your decisions will open or close doors. Each decision you make will increase or decrease you.

12. Miracles come easily to the obedient:

> *If ye be willing and obedient, ye shall eat the good of the land.*
>
> Isaiah 1:19

Any move toward self-sufficiency is a move away from God. So cultivate continuous gratefulness and thankfulness in your heart for the presence of the Holy Spirit in your life. Check His countenance. Pursue His approval:

> *The Lord make his face shine upon thee, and be gracious unto thee: the Lord lift up his countenance upon thee, and give thee peace.*
>
> Numbers 6:25,26

> *...Lord, lift thou up the light of thy countenance upon us.*
>
> Psalm 4:6

His countenance can be a very strong encouragement every moment of your life:

> *...hope thou in God: for I shall yet praise him for the help of his countenance.*
>
> Psalm 42:5

**Remember: miracles are coming toward you...or going past you...every day of your life.**

## You Will Succeed Only When Your Assignment Becomes an Obsession

### Focus Is Like a Magnet

Jesus Himself rebuked those who attempted to break His focus and obsession for completing the will of the Father.

> *But when he had turned about and looked on his disciples, he rebuked Peter, saying, Get thee behind me, Satan: for thou savourest not the things that be of God, but the things that be of men.*
>
> Mark 8:33

When you give your attention, time, and total effort to achieving your Assignment, you will experience extraordinary currents of favor and miracles. As we have seen, whatever has the ability to keep your attention, has mastered you.

The apostle Paul was obsessed with his Assignment. This explains his remarkable success in the face of enemies, adversaries, and even his friends who misunderstood him. It also explains his letter to the Philippians:

> *...this one thing I do, forgetting those things which are behind, and reaching forth unto those things which are before, I press toward the mark for the prize of the high calling of God in Christ Jesus.*
>
> Philippians 3:13,14

> Whatever has the ability to keep your attention, has mastered you.

Paul moved away from past hurts, failures, and memories. Obviously, he had a photograph of those things before him, and he understood the following five keys:

## DEVELOPING AN OBSESSION FOR YOUR ASSIGNMENT

1. Refuse any weight or distraction to your Assignment:

   > *... let us lay aside every weight, and the sin which doth so easily beset us, and let us run with patience the race that is set before us.*
   >
   > Hebrews 12:1

2. Be ruthless in severing any ties to a project not connected to your Assignment. As Paul instructed Timothy:

   > *No man that warreth entangleth himself with the affairs of this life; that he may please him who hath chosen him to be a soldier.*
   >
   > 2 Timothy 2:4

3. Constantly study your Assignment. As the apostle urged Timothy:

> *Study to shew thyself approved unto God, a workman that needeth not to be ashamed, rightly dividing the word of truth.*
>
> 2 Timothy 2:15

4.  Shun conversations that are unrelated to your Assignment:

> *But shun profane and vain babblings: for they increase unto more ungodliness... But foolish and unlearned questions avoid, knowing they do gender strife.*
>
> 2 Timothy 2:16, 23

5.  Learn to sever any relationship that does not feed your addiction to God's presence and your obsession to complete His Assignment in your life:

> *And if any man obey not our word by this epistle, note that man, and have no company with him, that he may be ashamed.*
>
> 2 Thessalonians 3:14

## SATAN DREADS THE COMPLETION OF YOUR ASSIGNMENT

Each act of obedience can destroy a thousand satanic plans.

I must share an experience with you. You will appreciate it because I am certain it will happen to you in your future (if it has not already happened.)

My secretary handed me the telephone number of a friend I had not seen for twenty-five years. He had not written, telephoned, or sown a seed into my ministry for that same amount of time. Then, suddenly one day he telephoned several times. Then he came to my weekly Bible study, sowed a generous seed into my ministry, and invited me to supper.

At supper, my old friend said, "Mike, I am making more than $20,000 a month. It is the most wonderful company I have ever been involved with. I want you to become a part of it with me."

"Well," I replied slowly, "I am very consumed with my ministry. I really do not have the time to develop a secondary income at this point in my life. But, I appreciate your offer."

He was stunned. "But I know that you are going to need a strong financial base when you retire in the future. It is easy," he said. "You know thousands of people. You do not have to do anything but ask me to come and present this multi-level marketing plan to your people. They will come because they know you personally. And, this product is the best on the market. People will always need this product. Your people need it."

Well, I was impressed with his $20,000 per month income, but I had to be very direct with him. So I said, "I like your product. I believe everyone should have it. I will buy one from you. And I will tell my friends about you. But I cannot get involved in selling them, because I cannot let this product consume my attention, efforts, and time. It would be impossible for me to develop an obsession with this product. You see, I know that I can only succeed with something that consumes and envelopes me. Besides that, I have not received an instruction from the Lord to pursue a business with this product."

My instructions had already arrived. My inner peace was proof that I was in the center of God's will with my Assignment. There will always be others who will have wonderful ideas and will offer you options other than your Assignment. But any hours you spend with them is a waste of their time and yours. I never heard from this man again.

You see, he had no interest in my Assignment whatsoever. He was only interested in my involvement with his dream. I was merely a vehicle to generate finances back into his own life.

My secretary handed me another telephone message recently. It was from a dear friend of mine who is well-known in ministry circles. He had built an incredible work for God, but because of extreme adversity had experienced some major losses in his personal life and ministry.

When I returned the call, he was eager to get some time with me. So I agreed to see him that night.

I could not imagine why this man wanted to meet with me so urgently. He had not telephoned me in the previous eight years. And now suddenly, seeing me was a matter of life and death.

When we met I found out that he was involved in a multi-level marketing program. He would succeed. I knew that. I also realized that anyone linked to him would also have significant success. He is a remarkable, brilliant, and enjoyable friend. But he had a different focus. So I was very direct when I said to him, "I really believe you could succeed significantly in this business. But, do you feel that this would distract you from the calling of God for ministry?"

"Oh, I will continue to have my ministry, but this will help people financially everywhere," he replied.

So I carefully said, "I will pray about it, of course. But, my obsession has become the Holy Spirit and spending time in *The Secret Place*. I have known more peace and joy since building my days around His presence than I have ever known in my lifetime. Financial freedom is wonderful, but doing the will of God and being in the center of my Assignment has become my obsession." I have not heard from him again.

When you insist on building your life around your Assignment, wrong relationships will die. Right relationships will be born. I have said it a thousand times — the best way to disconnect from wrong people is to become obsessed with doing the right thing. When your obsession is to do the right thing, wrong people will find you unbearable.

It is permissible for others to share their dreams. But it is disappointing to discover that they want nothing to do with you or your Assignment. It is rewarding to know that the Father will reward you one hundredfold for your obsession to do His plan. (See Mark 10:28-30.)

So fight for your focus. Battle hard. Build walls that strengthen your concentration. Ignore the jeers, laughter, and the criticism that you are "obsessed."

***Those who are obsessed with their Assignment rule this planet called earth.***

## FACT
## 15

## YOUR ASSIGNMENT
## REQUIRES PLANNING

### PLANNING IS OFTEN BURDENSOME

I am quite creative, and my friends know that I used to like to move suddenly. I dislike planning. It seems to take the spontaneity out of life. But now I like to think about things long before I do them. And I like to keep them in my mind. It is difficult and laborious to move my thoughts toward paper to allow my circle of counsel to analyze, evaluate, and even criticize my goals. But it is one of the common denominators of champions: They think ahead.

I recently read where the Chief Executive Officer of two hundred corporations invested the first one hour of each day in the meticulous planning of that twenty-four hour day. This man writes out his plans in detail on paper. I have never known anyone personally who spends that kind of time carefully planning a day.

Lee Iacocca, the legendary former head of Chrysler, said one of his greatest mentors insisted that any ideas Iacocca had were to be written out in detail on paper before he would consider them.

You see, anyone can get carried away in the climate of conversation. But when you are required to write out a detailed plan on paper, facts arise that were previously hidden. Truths are much easier to see. Problem areas emerge. Weaknesses become obvious. Anything cloudy becomes clear. And, questions are answered.

*Your Bible is a collection of plans.*

That is why the Scriptures teach, "...Write the vision, and make it plain upon tables, that he may run that readeth it" (Habakkuk 2:2). You see, your Bible is a collection of plans. God wanted you to see, observe, meditate upon, and visualize those plans.

The Bible is also a collection of champions who planned their successes ahead of time. Solomon had a plan for the temple. It was quite detailed (2 Chronicles 3-5). Noah was given a plan for the ark (Genesis 6:14-16). Moses was given a plan for the tabernacle (Exodus 36-40).

God even had detailed plans regarding offerings from the people! (See Leviticus 1-9.)

Great concert pianists invest many hours in practice before their concerts. The crowds hear only the results of their preparation. Now that you are serious about fulfilling your Assignment, it is time for you to invest some time into preparing for your performance. It is time to get serious about making your Assignment plans.

## 4 REWARDS OF PLANNING

1. Planning ahead eliminates stress in the difficult seasons of your life:

*Go to the ant, thou sluggard; consider her ways, and be wise: which having no guide, overseer, or ruler, provideth her meat in the summer, and gathereth her food in the harvest.*

Proverbs 6:6-8

2. Planning greatly affects the decisions you make:

*Or what king, going to make war against another king, sitteth not down first, and consulteth whether he be able with ten thousand to meet him that cometh against him with twenty thousand? Or else, while the other is yet a great way off, he sendeth an ambassage, and desireth conditions of peace.*

Luke 14:31,32

3. The quality of your preparation determines the quality of your performance:

*Seest thou a man diligent in his business? he shall stand before kings; he shall not stand before mean men.*

Proverbs 22:29

4. Proper planning guarantees completion of any project.

*For which of you, intending to build a tower, sitteth not down first, and counteth the cost, whether he hath sufficient to finish it? Lest haply, after he hath laid the foundation, and is not able to finish it, all that behold it begin to mock him, saying, This man began to build, and is not able to finish.*

Luke 14:28-30

Heavyweight boxing champions also plan many weeks before they fight. They prepare. They know their preparation is the only difference between winning and losing. I have often said such champions do not become champions in the ring. They are recognized in the ring. Their becoming champions occurred in their daily routine.

It seems that most of us have a dominant influence of either our mind or our heart. There are MIND people, and there are HEART people. MIND people are methodical, analytical and make decisions based on facts. HEART people appear more sensitive, more intuitive, and they lean toward spontaneity and flexibility.

- ■ MIND people desire *facts*.
- ■ HEART people desire *inspiration*.

Both kinds of people are necessary for completing your life Assignment. But it is my personal observation that MIND people often drift away from *The Secret Place*, because of their dependence upon academic studies and gathered data. And that HEART people often move away from mentorship and the written discoveries of others toward special revelation in their prayer time. So I have discovered the following two important principles that have helped me greatly in gaining a balance in these areas:

- ■ Praying does not replace *planning*.
- ■ Planning cannot replace *praying*.

Let me illustrate. Study Joshua and the two battles of Ai in Joshua 7. When Joshua did not consult the Lord, he lost the first battle and was devastated:

> *And Joshua rent his clothes, and fell to the earth upon his face before the ark of the Lord until the eventide, he and the elders of Israel, and put dust upon their heads.*
>
> Joshua 7:6

Israel had sinned. They had taken of the accursed things, and in their defeat, God was judging them. So when Joshua finally went to prayer, God instructed him to quit praying and told him, "Get thee up; wherefore liest thus upon thy face?" (Joshua 7:10.) This is one of the few times that God did not respond to prayer. Why?

God's plan had not been pursued. It was ignored. Obviously, an entire day of prayer could not replace the simplicity of the plan of God:

> *...to obey is better than sacrifice, and to hearken than the fat of rams.*
>
> 1 Samuel 15:22

After the sin of Achan was revealed and penalized, God spoke again. And Joshua was listening this time. God promised victory, but again, He stressed the importance of following a plan:

> *...only the spoil thereof, and the cattle thereof, shall ye take for a prey unto yourselves: lay thee an ambush for the city behind it.*
>
> Joshua 8:2

As this next passage reveals, Joshua had a meticulous plan, and won the second battle of Ai. But it is important to note that Joshua's praying did not replace his planning. His praying revealed the plan of God.

## THE 7 MOST IMPORTANT KEYS IN PLANNING

1 Ask God for wisdom. (See James 1:5.)

2. Keep a daily planner — a time management system. You can find them in office supply stores. Or you may secure a recommendation on one from someone you admire.

3. Keep your daily planner handy, and refer to it often. Using a planner is quite difficult at first, and may even seem to slow you down. But it will prove to be a valuable and necessary tool for long-term gain in your life.

4. Write your plan out in detail.

5. Follow it on a daily basis.

6. Develop a detailed picture of your desired end and conclusion.

7. Keep flexible for the unexpected, then adapt the plan accordingly.

Remember, it takes only a moment to get a command from God. But it takes a whole lifetime to receive the plan from Him.

I am learning to stay in *The Secret Place* past the moment of hearing a command from the Lord. Because when I linger in His presence, He begins to show me the plans for achieving and accomplishing those commands that He has imparted.

In a moment Noah heard, "Build an ark." But he had to linger longer to hear the details of building a safe ark and the plan for the inhabitants of it.

### 3 POWERFUL INGREDIENTS

There are therefore three powerful ingredients that produce a successful plan. First of all, your planning should begin with:

1. Time in *The Secret Place:*

> *He that dwelleth in the secret place of the most High shall abide under the shadow of the Almighty.*
>
> Psalm 91:1

Because your time in *The Secret Place* will determine your strength in the public place:

*But they that wait upon the Lord shall renew their strength; they shall mount up with wings as eagles; they shall run, and not be weary; they shall walk, and not faint.*

Isaiah 40:31

2. Second, your planning should involve your circle of counsel:

*Two are better than one; because they have a good reward for their labour.*

Ecclesiastes 4:9

Worthy advisors can help keep you safe from mistakes:

*Where no counsel is, the people fall: but in the multitude of counsellors there is safety.*

Proverbs 11:14

Because David was very wise himself, he knew how to tap into the mental capability and anointing of others:

*And of the children of Issachar, which were men that had understanding of the times, to know what Israel ought to do; the heads of them were two hundred; and all their brethren were at their commandment.*

1 Chronicles 12:32

3. And third, your planning should involve the constant consulting of your lifetime Mentor, the Holy Spirit:

*But the Comforter, which is the Holy Ghost, whom the Father will send in my name, he shall teach you all things, and bring all things to your remembrance, whatsoever I have said unto you.*

John 14:26

A closing note. Think about it: The Marriage Supper of the Lamb has been planned for more than six thousand years now. Just imagine the splendor, the majesty, and the memory it will create!

*The more thorough the plan, the more successful and the longer your memory of the event will last.*

# FACT 16

## YOUR ASSIGNMENT MAY REQUIRE SEASONS OF WAITING

### WAITING ON GOD IS PROOF OF TRUST

Waiting also provides God time to address the problems we encounter as Christians in life — miraculously. God is a miracle God. But when you get ahead of Him, you rob Him of an opportunity to prove His power in your life. So learn to wait.

### 13 REWARDS FOR WAITING ON GOD

1. Waiting reveals patience. Patience is a seed that always produces a desired harvest. Patience is always rewarded:

> *In your patience possess ye your souls.*
>
> Luke 21:19

> *Through faith also Sara herself received strength to conceive seed, and was delivered of a child when she was past age, because she judged him faithful who had promised.*
>
> Hebrews 11:11

2. Waiting time is not wasted time:

*But let patience have her perfect work, that ye may be perfect and entire, wanting nothing.*

James 1:4

3. Waiting guarantees favorable results:

*The Lord is good unto them that wait for him, to the soul that seeketh him. It is good that a man should both hope and quietly wait for the salvation of the Lord.*

Lamentations 3:25,26

> Your flesh will react to waiting. It hates waiting. It wants action.

4. Waiting is learning time. As long as you are learning, you are not losing. Your Assignment will require warfare. Battles are normal on the field of your Assignment. The integrity of the general demands that he qualify his soldiers for the battle. God will train and teach you in the waiting time:

*Blessed be the Lord my strength, which teacheth my hands to war and my fingers to fight.*

Psalm 144:1

Your flesh will react to waiting. It hates waiting. It wants action. It pursues activity. Waiting forces your flesh to die.

5. Waiting will reveal the true motives and intentions of those around you. Motives are not always easily discerned. This is why Joseph was willing to wait before revealing his identity to his brothers when they approached him for food during a famine in the land.

Joseph's brothers did not know he was related to them. He knew them. Undoubtedly, the desire to reveal himself was intense. But he knew the limitations of intuition. He remembered the excitement of sharing his dream with his brothers only to be sold into slavery because of it.

Wise men never trust their intuition — they rely on tests.

■ The young *trust*.

■ The wise *test*.

6. Waiting reveals that you trust God, but are willing to test men. It is biblical:

> *Some trust in chariots, and some in horses: but we will remember the name of the Lord our God.*
>
> Psalm 20:7

You see, the wrong people can keep their mistakes covered for long periods of time, but waiting forces the truth to emerge.

7. Waiting enables you to gather accurate and untainted information. The quality of your information determines the quality of your decisions. And the quality of your decisions determines the quality of your life.

8. Waiting brings you truth.

9. More waiting brings you more truth.

10. Enough waiting brings you enough truth.

11. You will never see the hand of God if you keep trusting the hand of man in your life. Unwillingness to wait for supernatural provision will produce tragedies every time.

If you could have attended a workshop of Abraham, you would have heard him weep and tell you a thousand times, "Do not birth an Ishmael in your life. Wait for the timing of God. He will always fulfill His promise."

Your Father knows you very well. He is not faint. He is not weary. There is no limit to His understanding.

12. Waiting increases strength:

*He giveth power to the faint; and to them that have no might he increaseth strength. Even the youths shall faint and be weary, and the young men shall utterly fall: but they that wait upon the Lord shall renew their strength; they shall mount up with wings as eagles; they shall run, and not be weary; and they shall walk, and not faint.*

Isaiah 40:29-31

13. Waiting is a weapon Satan dreads for you to ever discover:

*Lest Satan should get an advantage of us: for we are not ignorant of his devices.*

2 Corinthians 2:11

*Waiting on God's timing will produce the desired results of your Assignment.*

# FACT
# 17

## Your Assignment
## Will Be Revealed Progressively

### Your Puzzle Is Revealed Piece by Piece

Each day produces new clues to your Assignment. Philip experienced his instructions from the Holy Spirit piece by piece. First:

> *The angel of the Lord spake unto Philip, saying, Arise, and go toward the south unto the way that goeth down from Jerusalem unto Gaza, which is desert.*
>
> Acts 8:26

You will not receive an understanding of your entire Assignment during one visit with God. He is interested in relationship, not an event. He requires continuous exchange with Him. He imparts information in paragraphs, not in chapters:

> *But the word of the Lord was unto them precept upon precept, precept upon precept; line upon line, line upon line; here a little, and there a little....*
>
> Isaiah 28:13

So Philip went. When he arrived, he noticed a eunuch sitting in a chariot. This Ethiopian, the treasurer for Candace the queen of the Ethiopians, was reading Isaiah. Then another instruction came:

> *Then the Spirit said unto Philip, Go near, and join thyself to this chariot.*
>
> Acts 8:29

> You will not receive an understanding of your entire Assignment during one visit with God.

Then after the eunuch was baptized, Philip received another instruction, and "Philip was found at Azotus: and passing through he preached in all the cities, till he came to Caesarea" (Acts 8:40).

## WHAT YOU DO FIRST DETERMINES WHAT GOD REVEALS NEXT

When I was a young minister, I wanted God to give me a total photograph of my journey and its conclusion. I fasted for it. I prayed for it. I even pursued the advice of other worthy mentors. But it never happened. Somebody has called it, "One day at a time." It takes hourly dependence upon the Holy Spirit to develop the relationship that He desires with you.

Moses understood this principle very well. True, it became discouraging at times, but it kept him linked to God and dependent upon Him. Moses watched as God sent each plague upon the Egyptians, from the dying of the fish, to the coming of the frogs, lice and flies, to the death of the cattle, then the downpour of fiery hail and the swarms of locusts — like a collection of seasons. (See Exodus 7-10.)

## THE SMALLEST INSTRUCTION HAS A PURPOSE

You will not always understand it. You may even wish and pray for more. But His method of measuring out instructions is to increase your faith step by step. It is similar to a weight trainer who carefully and patiently works a young man from lifting 50 pounds on the bench press, to eventually lifting 150 pounds. Had he demanded and required the full weight at the beginning, the young man would have become debilitated, demoralized, discouraged, and depressed. He would have quit.

But the trainer places just enough stress and expectation to grow small levels of strength, confidence, and expectation. Remember this Wisdom Key —

## YOU CAN GO ANYWHERE YOU WANT TO GO IF YOU ARE WILLING TO TAKE ENOUGH SMALL STEPS

Instructions are seasonal. That is why God used the cloud and the fire to guide Moses:

> *...thy cloud standeth over them, and that thou goest before them, by day time in a pillar of a cloud, and in a pillar of fire by night.*
>
> Numbers 14:14

Receiving instructions from the Holy Spirit reminds me much of the Israelites' gathering of the manna. Each morning required a fresh pursuit. It was only during the Sabbath that He provided any extra to be stored. He wanted them to stay in a continuous attitude of thanksgiving. He desired total addiction to His presence and an awareness of His importance.

In my own personal life, it has been impossible to gather up a stack of instructions for the years ahead. The Holy Spirit requires continuous pursuit. So the message of the manna is: every morning you must enter *The Secret Place* for fresh instructions for that very day.

Also, what you do first determines what God will do second. When I complete His first instruction, I become qualified for His second instruction:

> *But seek ye first the kingdom of God, and his righteousness; and all these things shall be added unto you.*
>
> Matthew 6:33

Keep listening for His voice. The Holy Spirit is talking to you:

> *And thine ears shall hear a word behind thee, saying, This is the way, walk ye in it, when ye turn to the right hand, and when ye turn to the left.*
>
> Isaiah 30:21

**Never forget that you will never progress beyond your last point of disobedience.**

# YOUR ASSIGNMENT WILL CONTAIN SEASONS OF SOCIAL ISOLATION AND CHANGE

## THE PURPOSE OF ISOLATION IS TO BIRTH A TOTAL FOCUS ON GOD

You see, the only reason men fail is broken focus. When Satan wants to distract you, he brings someone into your life to break your attention off of God. So the Father in His incredible wisdom knows how to remove those distractions and cause us to behold Him again.

You may experience spiritual isolation from someone who labors with you in the work of God:

*For Demas hath forsaken me, having loved this present world, and is departed unto Thessalonica....*

2 Timothy 4:10

You may experience social isolation and loss of respect in your community:

> *By faith Moses, when he was come to years, refused to be called the son of Pharaoh's daughter; choosing rather to suffer affliction with the people of God, than to enjoy the pleasures of sin for a season; esteeming the reproach of Christ greater riches than the treasures in Egypt: for he had respect unto the recompence of the reward.*
>
> Hebrews 11:24-26

> *Endurance is rewarded. Always.*

You may experience bankruptcy and financial isolation from everything that was secure in your life. It happened to Job:

> *And there came a messenger unto Job, and said, The oxen were plowing, and the asses feeding beside them: and the Sabeans fell upon them, and carried them away; yea, they have slain the servants with the edge of the sword....*
>
> Job 1:14,15

> *While he was yet speaking, there came also another, and said, The Chaldeans made out three bands, and fell upon the camels, and have carried them away....*
>
> Job 1:17

## 4 FOCUS KEYS FOR WHEN YOUR SEASONS OF LIFE CHANGE

1. The seasons will change:

> *And the Lord turned the captivity of Job, when he prayed for his friends: also the Lord gave Job twice as much as he had before.*
>
> Job 42:10

2. Endurance is rewarded. Always. That is why Paul encouraged:

> *Cast not away therefore your confidence, which hath great recompence of reward. For ye have need of patience, that, after ye have done the will of God, ye might receive the promise.*
>
> Hebrews 10:35,36

3. God reveals the purpose of seasons:

> *And thou shalt remember all the way which the Lord thy God led thee these forty years in the wilderness, to humble thee, and to prove thee, to know what was in thine heart, whether thou wouldest keep his commandments, or no...that he might make thee know that man doth not live by bread only, but by every word that proceedeth out of the mouth of the Lord doth man live.*
>
> Deuteronomy 8:2,3

4. Your next season will be a season of blessing. God guaranteed it:

> *For the Lord thy God bringeth thee into a good land, a land of brooks of water, of fountains and depths that spring out of valleys and hills; a land of wheat, and barley, and vines, and fig trees, and pomegranates; a land of oil olive, and honey; a land wherein thou shalt eat bread without scarceness, thou shalt not lack any thing in it....*
>
> Deuteronomy 8:7-9

*He did it for Israel. He will do it for you.*

# FACT 19

## NEVER STAY WHERE YOU HAVE NOT BEEN ASSIGNED

### YOU ARE NOT ASSIGNED EVERYWHERE

I was speaking at a church up North. I had been there for two days, and the atmosphere in the church was as dead as it is at four o'clock in the morning. There is a great difference between holy quietness and deathly silence — and these people were deathly silent!

But I persisted, because truth planted can change lives. The people kept looking at me like they did not understand a word I was saying. They stared at me. But I did not give up, although I was dying inside. Every word was torturous as I kept teaching the Word, thinking that it would eventually take root.

Finally, I stopped and asked everyone to bow their head in prayer. "Father," I prayed, "what in the world is wrong here?"

"This was your schedule," He replied.

So I asked the people to stand to their feet. Then I explained to them, "I realize that we are supposed to continue here until tomorrow night. However, I have noticed in the last two days of ministry that you have just stared at me. You have never shown any response. No truth I share seems to ignite you or encourage you. You stare at me as though I just landed from Neptune. I do not think you understand anything I am saying to you. Well, I have just asked the Lord why, and He told me that this place, this church, was not even His Assignment for me...it is something I chose on my own. So I am going back to Dallas. I will not be back tomorrow night. God bless you folks!" And I went home.

> *Jesus did not go where He was needed. He went where He was wanted.*

Some would find that intolerable. However, I am certain if you would become more careful in where you sow your seed of energy, your seed of love and time, your seed of knowledge...that you will see great differences in the results of your life.

Jesus did not go where He was needed. He went where He was wanted. He taught His disciples:

> *And whosoever shall not receive you, nor hear your words, when ye depart out of that house or city, shake off the dust of your feet.*
>
> Matthew 10:14

## GO WHERE YOU ARE CELEBRATED, NOT TOLERATED

Certainly, there will be moments when your own assessment of your labor will be inaccurate. There will be times when you think your work is totally in vain, only to find out through a little more tenacity and determination that the winds of God were preparing to blow. His blessings were about to come.

There is a difference between pouring your life out at the specific place where God assigns you and where you assign yourself.

*So remember: you do not have to stay where God has not assigned you.*

**FACT 20**

## CRISIS IS A NORMAL EVENT ON THE ROAD TO YOUR ASSIGNMENT

### CRISIS NEVER SURPRISES GOD

Actually if anybody is ever really doing anything in the kingdom of God, crises are to be expected occasionally.

Peter believed this:

> *Beloved, think it not strange concerning the fiery trial which is to try you, as though some strange thing happened unto you: but rejoice, inasmuch as ye are partakers of Christ's sufferings; that, when his glory shall be revealed, ye may be glad also with exceeding joy.*

1 Peter 4:12,13

So here are twenty important facts to remember during crisis.

### 20 CRISIS FACTS

1. Every champion in Scripture seemed to move continuously from one crisis to another.

*But in all things approving ourselves as the ministers of God, in much patience, in afflictions, in necessities, in distresses, in stripes, in imprisonments, in tumults, in labours, in watchings, in fastings.*

2 Corinthians 6:4,5

2. Paul experienced highs and lows in favor and disfavor:

*By honour and dishonour, by evil report and good report: as deceivers, and yet true; as unknown, and yet well known; as dying, and, behold, we live; as chastened, and not killed; as sorrowful, yet always rejoicing; as poor, yet making many rich; as having nothing, and yet possessing all things.*

2 Corinthians 6:8-10

> Every champion in Scripture seemed to move continuously from one crisis to another.

3. Jesus experienced numerous crises. It finally seemed to end at the crucifixion. Yet, even at His crucifixion, He was jeered and taunted by His enemies. Even His resurrection has been doubted by thousands. (See Matthew 27:40-43.)

4. Crisis is always the hinge on the door of promotion. Every champion has had difficult circumstances to overcome.

- Daniel was thrown into the lions' den.
- Daniel's three friends, Shadrach, Meshach, and Abed-nego, were thrown into the fiery furnace.
- Job lost his children, possessions, and good health.
- Elijah's brook dried up.
- The widow of Zarephath came to her last meal during the famine, almost starving.

■ Joseph experienced hatred by his brothers, false accusation against his character, then was forgotten in prison for two years after he interpreted the dream of the butler.

■ Isaac had one foolish son, Esau, and a deceptive, manipulative son named Jacob.

A visit to a teaching workshop would benefit us. Picture this scenario. Pause for a moment and revisit the workshop where a world-renowned missionary evangelist is speaking. The place is crammed with young preachers who are excited about the revelation imparted through this man. When you walk through the door, you are looking for a tall, good-looking and powerfully built man with exquisite stature and dynamic magnetism. You ask for him, but they point to a squinty-eyed, short, bowlegged man speaking from the platform. The man is Paul.

Listen to him:

*Are they ministers of Christ? (I speak as a fool) I am more; in labours more abundant, in stripes above measure, in prisons more frequent, in deaths oft. Of the Jews five times received I forty stripes save one. Thrice was I beaten with rods, once was I stoned, thrice I suffered shipwreck, a night and a day I have been in the deep; in journeyings often, in perils of waters, in perils of robbers, in perils by mine own countrymen, in perils by the heathen, in perils in the city, in the wilderness, in perils in the sea, in perils among false brethren; in weariness and painfulness, in watchings often, in hunger and thirst, in fastings often, in cold and nakedness. Beside those things that are without, that which cometh upon me daily, the care of all the churches. Who is weak, and I am not weak? Who is offended, and I burn not?*

2 Corinthians 11:23-29

Paul is not complaining in this passage. He is exultant!

*If I must needs glory, I will glory of the things which concern mine infirmities.*

2 Corinthians 11:30

5. Paul knew that a crisis attracted the power and strength of God. He continues:

*And he said unto me, My grace is sufficient for thee: for my strength is made perfect in weakness. Most gladly therefore will I rather glory in my infirmities, that the power of Christ may rest upon me. Therefore I take pleasure in infirmities, in reproaches, in necessities, in persecutions, in distresses for Christ's sake: for when I am weak, then am I strong.*

2 Corinthians 12:9,10

6. Paul embraced his seasons of crises:

*If we suffer, we shall also reign with him....*

2 Timothy 2:12

*...if so be that we suffer with him, that we may be also glorified together. For I reckon that the sufferings of this present time are not worthy to be compared with the glory which shall be revealed in us.*

Romans 8:17,18

7. Paul anticipated recognition and reward for surviving his crises. His voice was filled with energy, excitement, and joy:

*I have fought a good fight, I have finished my course, I have kept the faith: henceforth there is laid up for me a crown of righteousness, which the Lord, the righteous judge, shall give me at that day: and not to me only, but unto all them also that love his appearing.*

2 Timothy 4:7,8

8. Paul remembered when his difficult days were caused by ignorance instead of working with God to birth his promotion:

*For we ourselves also were sometimes foolish, disobedient, deceived, serving divers lusts and pleasures, living in malice and envy, hateful, and hating one another. But after that the kindness and love of God our Saviour toward man appeared, not by works of righteousness which we have done, but according to his mercy he saved us, by the washing of regeneration, and renewing of the Holy Ghost; which he shed on us abundantly through Jesus Christ our Saviour; that being justified by his grace, we should be made heirs according to the hope of eternal life.*

Titus 3:3-7

9. Paul encouraged us to look beyond the present crisis:

*Looking for that blessed hope, and the glorious appearing of the great God and our Saviour Jesus Christ.*

Titus 2:13

10. The apostle Peter also understood what was on the other side of suffering and crisis:

*But rejoice, inasmuch as ye are partakers of Christ's sufferings; that, when his glory shall be revealed, ye may be glad also with exceeding joy. If ye be reproached for the name of Christ, happy are ye; for the spirit of glory and of God resteth upon you: on their part he is evil spoken of, but on your part he is glorified.*

1 Peter 4:13,14

11. James saw the crown of life that lay beyond crisis:

> *Blessed is the man that endureth temptation: for when he is tried, he shall receive the crown of life, which the Lord hath promised to them that love him.*
>
> James 1:12

12. James understood that crisis produces patience:

> *Knowing this, that the trying of your faith worketh patience.*
>
> James 1:3

13. And James knew that patience could produce every miracle and desired provision you could ever want:

> *But let patience have her perfect work, that ye may be perfect and entire, wanting nothing.*
>
> James 1:4

14. Be encouraged in knowing that you will have a divine companion through every crisis:

> *...Fear not: for I have redeemed thee, I have called thee by thy name; thou art mine. When thou passest through the waters, I will be with thee; and through the rivers, they shall not overflow thee: when thou walkest through the fire, thou shalt not be burned; neither shall the flame kindle upon thee.*
>
> Isaiah 43:1,2

15. Your crisis will pass:

> *For his anger endureth but a moment; in his favour is life: weeping may endure for a night, but joy cometh in the morning.*
>
> Psalm 30:5

16. Learn to picture the rewards beyond crisis:

> *Now no chastening for the present seemeth to be joyous, but grievous: nevertheless afterward it yieldeth the peaceable fruit of righteousness unto them which are exercised thereby. Wherefore lift up the hands which hang down, and the feeble knees; and make straight paths for your feet, lest that which is lame be turned out of the way; but let it rather be healed.*
>
> Hebrews 12:11-13

17. Never discuss the problems of your crises with someone incapable of solving them:

> *A fool uttereth all his mind: but a wise man keepeth it in till afterwards.*
>
> Proverbs 29:11

18. You will learn more in crisis than you will ever learn in any victory:

> *Though he were a Son, yet learned he obedience by the things which he suffered.*
>
> Hebrews 5:8

19. Crisis is the season in which God has an opportunity to reveal His love and supernatural power in your life:

> *And he said unto me, My grace is sufficient for thee: for my strength is made perfect in weakness. Most gladly therefore will I rather glory in my infirmities, that the power of Christ may rest upon me. Therefore I take pleasure in infirmities, in reproaches, in necessities, in persecutions, in distresses for Christ's sake: for when I am weak, then am I strong.*
>
> 2 Corinthians 12:9,10

20. In every crisis, increasing your time spent in *The Secret Place*, your prayer closet, will bring protection:

> *For in the time of trouble he shall hide me in his pavilion: in the secret of his tabernacle shall he hide me; he shall set me up upon a rock. And now shall mine head be lifted up above mine enemies round about me: therefore will I offer in his tabernacle sacrifices of joy; I will sing, yea, I will sing praises unto the Lord.*
>
> Psalm 27:5,6

*Crisis is always an exit from your present...it is your passage to promotion.*

# FACT
# 21

## YOUR ASSIGNMENT MAY REQUIRE SEASONS OF INTENSIFIED PRAYER AND FASTING

### CHAMPIONS USE THE WEAPON OF FASTING

The purpose of fasting is not to destroy your health. It is to deprive yourself of something you love — to move the hand of God to provide something you do not have.

I have fasted three days a week many times throughout my ministry and life. And I have learned some powerful lessons because of the discipline. I have discovered the importance of total focus during meal times. It is sometimes better to withdraw from the company of friends who are enjoying a meal around a restaurant table — to focus instead on a private time of prayer with Him.

Various fasts are possible. Some people fast from food and water for three days. Others drink water, but fast from food for up to seven, twenty-one, and even forty days. The important thing is to be led by the voice of the Holy Spirit. (It is always wise to have a physician oversee fasts for the purpose of keeping your health strong.)

## UNUSUAL WARFARE REQUIRES
## UNUSUAL WEAPONS

Jesus embraced prayer and fasting as effective weapons. Demon powers always succumb to these weapons. I am so thankful that the body of Christ is awakening again and becoming aware of the remarkable influence we can have when we pray and set aside time to fast.

> *Jesus embraced prayer and fasting as effective weapons.*

## 23 IMPORTANT FACTS
## ABOUT FASTING

1. God commanded us to fast:

*Therefore also now, saith the Lord, turn ye even to me with all your heart, and with fasting, and with weeping, and with mourning: and rend your heart, and not your garments, and turn unto the Lord your God: for he is gracious and merciful, slow to anger, and of great kindness, and repenteth him of the evil.*

Joel 2:12,13

2. Fasting is a force in the spirit world. When the disciples could not cast out the dumb and deaf spirit of the young son, they asked Jesus:

*Why could not we cast him out? And he said unto them, This kind can come forth by nothing, but by prayer and fasting.*

Mark 9:28,29

*Then was Jesus led up of the Spirit into the wilderness to be tempted of the devil. And when he had fasted forty days and forty nights, he was afterward an hungered.*

Matthew 4:1,2

3. You should fast during important decision making and between major events of your life. Jesus did. When Jesus was baptized by John in the Jordan River, Jesus saw:

> *...the Spirit of God descending like a dove, and lighting upon him: and lo a voice from heaven, saying, This is my beloved Son, in whom I am well pleased.*

Matthew 3:16,17

Then Jesus fasted. Then, after fasting, He selected His disciples:

> *And Jesus, walking by the sea of Galilee, saw two brethren, Simon called Peter, and Andrew his brother, casting a net into the sea: for they were fishers. And he saith unto them, Follow me, and I will make you fishers of men. And they straightway left their nets, and followed him. And going on from thence, he saw other two brethren, James the son of Zebedee, and John his brother, in a ship with Zebedee their father, mending their nets; and he called them. And they immediately left the ship and their father, and followed him.*

Matthew 4:18-22

4. You should fast to affect the decision of God in the crises of those you love. David did:

> *David therefore besought God for the child; and David fasted, and went in, and lay all night upon the earth. And the elders of his house arose, and went to him, to raise him up from the earth: but he would not, neither did he eat bread with them.*

2 Samuel 12:16,17

121

5. You should fast habitually. Anna did. This 84-year-old widow and prophetess never left the temple, and fasted continuously:

> *And she was a widow of about fourscore and four years, which departed not from the temple, but served God with fastings and prayers night and day.*
>
> Luke 2:37

6. Your fasting follows the examples of great champions. The apostle Paul fasted:

> *But in all things approving ourselves as the ministers of God, in much patience, in afflictions, in necessities, in distresses, in stripes, in imprisonments, in tumults, in labours, in watchings, in fastings.*
>
> 2 Corinthians 6:4,5

7. You should fast often, regardless of outward conditions:

> *In weariness and painfulness, in watchings often, in hunger and thirst, in fastings often, in cold and nakedness.*
>
> 2 Corinthians 11:27

8. You should fast for the healing of your children. David did:

> *David therefore besought God for the child; and David fasted, and went in, and lay all night upon the earth. And the elders of his house arose, and went to him, to raise him up from the earth: but he would not, neither did he eat bread with them.*
>
> 2 Samuel 12:16,17

9. You should fast to create favor in a political crisis. Esther did. She requested that her employees, and many others, join her in a food and drink fast for three days:

> *Then Esther bade them return Mordecai this answer,*
> *Go, gather together all the Jews that are present in Shushan,*
> *and fast ye for me, and neither eat nor drink three days,*
> *night or day: I also and my maidens will fast likewise....*
>
> Esther 4:15,16

10. You should fast to create acceptance and influence with those in leadership and positions of power. Queen Esther did:

> *Then Esther bade them return Mordecai this answer,*
> *Go, gather together all the Jews that are present in Shushan,*
> *and fast ye for me, and neither eat nor drink three days,*
> *night or day: I also and my maidens will fast likewise; and*
> *so will I go in unto the king, which is not according to the*
> *law: and if I perish, I perish.*
>
> Esther 4:15,16

11. You should fast during times of unusual attack and isolation. David did:

> *When I wept, and chastened my soul with fasting, that*
> *was to my reproach.*
>
> Psalm 69:10

12. Your fasting will produce humility:

> *...I humbled my soul with fasting....*
>
> Psalm 35:13

13. You should fast to influence three areas of your life as Ezra the priest did for his:

    1. Direction
    2. Family
    3. Finances

> *Then I proclaimed a fast there, at the river of Ahava, that*
> *we might afflict ourselves before our God, to seek of him a*
> *right way for us, and for our little ones, and for all our*
> *substance.*
>
> Ezra 8:21

14. Your fasting is wasted effort if you lack integrity or proper motives:

> *Then said the Lord unto me, Pray not for this people for*
> *their good. When they fast, I will not hear their cry; and*
> *when they offer burnt offering and an oblation, I will not*
> *accept them: but I will consume them by the sword, and by*
> *the famine, and by the pestilence.*
>
> Jeremiah 14:11,12

15. You should fast to avert the judgments of God upon your life:

> *Sanctify ye a fast, call a solemn assembly...for the day*
> *of the Lord is at hand, and as a destruction from the*
> *Almighty shall it come.*
>
> Joel 1:14,15

16. Your fasting affects your supernatural provision:

> *Blow the trumpet in Zion, sanctify a fast.... Yea, the Lord*
> *will answer and say unto his people, Behold, I will send you*
> *corn, and wine, and oil, and ye shall be satisfied therewith:*
> *and I will no more make you a reproach among the heathen.*
>
> Joel 2:15,19

17. Your fasting is wrong if it is done publicly to impress other people about your spirituality:

*And when thou prayest, thou shalt not be as the hypocrites are: for they love to pray standing in the synagogues and in the corners of the streets, that they may be seen of men...Moreover when ye fast, be not, as the hypocrites, of a sad countenance: for they disfigure their faces, that they may appear unto men to fast....*

Matthew 6:5,16

18. Your fasting should be a private and silent posture before God:

*But thou, when thou fastest, anoint thine head, and wash thy face; that thou appear not unto men to fast, but unto thy Father which is in secret.*

Matthew 6:17

19. Your heavenly Father guarantees to reward you openly for private fasting:

*...and thy Father, which seeth in secret, shall reward thee openly.*

Matthew 6:18

20. Your fasting moves God to destroy your enemy:

*Blow the trumpet in Zion, sanctify a fast, call a solemn assembly...and I will no more make you a reproach among the heathen: but I will remove far off from you the northern army, and will drive him into a land barren and desolate, with his face toward the east sea, and his hinder part toward the utmost sea, and his stink shall come up, and his ill savour shall come up, because he hath done great things.*

Joel 2:15,19,20

21. Your fasting can birth a season of restoration after loss:

> *Blow the trumpet in Zion, sanctify a fast, call a solemn assembly...and he will cause to come down for you the rain, the former rain, and the latter rain in the first month. And the floors shall be full of wheat, and the vats shall overflow with wine and oil. And I will restore to you the years that the locust hath eaten, the cankerworm, and the caterpillar, and the palmerworm, my great army which I sent among you. And ye shall eat in plenty, and be satisfied, and praise the name of the Lord your God, that hath dealt wondrously with you: and my people shall never be ashamed.*
>
> Joel 2:15,23-26

22. Your fasting can birth an extraordinary experience with the Holy Spirit:

> *Blow the trumpet of Zion, sanctify a fast, call a solemn assembly... And it shall come to pass afterward, that I will pour out my spirit upon all flesh; and your sons and your daughters shall prophesy, your old men shall dream dreams, your young men shall see visions: and also upon the servants and upon the handmaids in those days will I pour out my spirit.*
>
> Joel 2:15,28,29

23. The geographical location for your Assignment can be revealed following a fast:

> *As they ministered to the Lord, and fasted, the Holy Ghost said, Separate Me Barnabas and Saul for the work whereunto I have called them. And when they had fasted and prayed, and laid their hands on them, they sent them*

*away. So they, being sent forth by the Holy Ghost, departed unto Seleucia; and from thence they sailed to Cyprus.*

Acts 13:2-4

The same Holy Spirit Who revealed the city and country of Paul and Barnabas' Assignment following their fast is not a respecter of persons. He will honor your seed of love and deprivation as you "minister to" and "fast," as Paul and Barnabas did, unto the Lord.

Every champion of faith knows the power of prayer. Those who embrace the extra weapon of fasting see increased results beyond their imagination.

## 10 KEYS TO EFFECTIVE PRAYING THAT WILL PRODUCE THE RESULTS YOU NEED

1. Do not attempt to pray for anything until you have forgiven those who have wronged you:

   *And when ye stand praying, forgive, if ye have ought against any: that your Father also which is in heaven may forgive you your trespasses. But if ye do not forgive, neither will your Father which is in heaven forgive your trespasses.*

   Mark 11:25,26

2. You must completely believe in your heart what you are praying with your mouth:

   *For verily I say unto you, That whosoever shall say unto this mountain, Be thou removed, and be thou cast into the sea; and shall not doubt in his heart, but shall believe that those things which he saith shall come to pass; he shall have whatsoever he saith. Therefore I say unto you, What things soever ye desire, when ye pray, believe that ye receive them, and ye shall have them.*

Mark 11:23,24

3. Prayer must be continuous and receive your total focus:

*But we will give ourselves continually to prayer, and to the ministry of the word.*

Acts 6:4

4. Unkindness and disrespect to your family members can hinder the results of your prayers:

*Likewise, ye husbands, dwell with them according to knowledge, giving honour unto the wife, as unto the weaker vessel, and as being heirs together of the grace of life; that your prayers be not hindered.*

1 Peter 3:7

5. The prayers of your mentors and spiritual leaders are especially effective when you pursue them:

*Is any sick among you? let him call for the elders of the church; and let them pray over him, anointing him with oil in the name of the Lord: and the prayer of faith shall save the sick, and the Lord shall raise him up; and if he hath committed sins, they shall be forgiven him. Confess your faults one to another, and pray one for another, that ye may be healed. The effectual fervent prayer of a righteous man availeth much.*

James 5:14-16

So pursue the prayer of agreement with those who have spiritual oversight in your life. There is a difference.

6. Your personal intercession for your leaders can produce miraculous change:

> *Peter therefore was kept in prison: but prayer was made without ceasing of the church unto God for him.*
>
> Acts 12:5

And as you know, the angel of the Lord came, and the chains fell off Peter's hands as he was set free from the prison.

7. You should have a special place for daily prayer. I call the special room where I meet with the Holy Spirit each day, *The Secret Place.* I have altars around the room. I keep an open Bible, legal pads and pens, and a cassette recorder to tape my notes. It is my daily appointment with God. It is the most important part of every day.

8. Your appointment with Him should be specific, at a certain time every day. There is power in routine and rhythm. It is the most difficult thing you will ever birth in your Christian life. Your time with the Holy Spirit in private prayer is the most powerful weapon you have against Satan. The secret of your future is hidden in your daily routine.

9. Music plays an important part in *The Secret Place.* Keep praise and worship continuously playing on music cassettes or CDs. Sing new songs to the Lord, as the Holy Spirit inspires you:

> *...come before his presence with singing... Enter into his gates with thanksgiving, and into his courts with praise....*
>
> Psalm 100:2,4

10. Learn to pray in the language of the Holy Spirit and interpret back what He is instructing:

*Wherefore let him that speaketh in an unknown tongue pray that he may interpret. For if I pray in an unknown tongue, my spirit prayeth, but my understanding is unfruitful. What is it then? I will pray with the spirit, and I will pray with the understanding also: I will sing with the spirit, and I will sing with the understanding also.*

1 Corinthians 14:13-15

**Your Assignment will always require His presence.**

## FACT 22

# THE COMPLETION OF YOUR ASSIGNMENT IS YOUR ENEMY'S GREATEST FEAR

### SATAN HATES FINISHERS

It is not enough to begin. Only those who endure to the end will be saved, promoted, and rewarded. That is why Satan deceives. If he can get one of God's children to forsake their Assignment before it is finished, he knows another Assignment may never begin. Or worse, he will fool you into thinking the unfinished Assignment was faithfully finished — making room for even more compromise in the days ahead.

So here are twenty-four encouragement keys that will help you finish and complete the Assignment God has birthed in your heart.

### 24 ASSIGNMENT COMPLETION KEYS

1. Jesus was a Finisher. When He died on Calvary, He cried:

> *It is finished: and he bowed his head, and gave up the ghost.*
> John 19:30

Jesus prayed this to the Father:

> *I have glorified thee on the earth: I have finished the work which thou gavest me to do.*
>
> John 17:4

2. Jesus is even called a FINISHER:

> *Looking unto Jesus the author and finisher of our faith; who for the joy that was set before him endured the cross, despising the shame, and is set down at the right hand of the throne of God.*
>
> Hebrews 12:2

*Jesus considered non-finishers to be disqualified for the kingdom.*

3. Jesus' OBSESSION was to FINISH. He wanted to reach the conclusion of His Assignment on earth. He thought it. He talked it. He lived it:

> *Jesus saith unto them, My meat is to do the will of him that sent me, and to finish his work.*
>
> John 4:34

4. Jesus considered non-finishers to be disqualified for the kingdom:

> *And Jesus said unto him, No man, having put his hand to the plough, and looking back, is fit for the kingdom of God.*
>
> Luke 9:62

5. The apostle Paul was a FINISHER:

> *I have fought a good fight, I have finished my course, I have kept the faith.*
>
> 2 Timothy 4:7

6. Nehemiah was a FINISHER:

> *So the wall was finished in the twenty and fifth day of the month Elul, in fifty and two days.*
>
> Nehemiah 6:15

7. Solomon was a FINISHER:

> *Thus Solomon finished the house of the Lord, and the king's house....*
>
> 2 Chronicles 7:11

8. Satan always attacks in seasons. It seems that he attacks when something is being birthed in your life that is very important. It may be the birth of your ministry, the birth of a new revelation from God, or the birth of a child in your home whom God will use as a champion. It may be the beginning of a physical or financial miracle.

9. Satan cannot foretell everything, or he might never have rebelled against God to begin with. But it does appear that, in the spirit world, information is discerned and processed. So when one of your children seems to be the "troublemaker" in your family, understand that this child may be experiencing mental attacks by demonic spirits more than all of the other children combined. So protect the child in your home who attracts more demonic attention than all of the other children combined. That child has an invisible Assignment that hell has discerned and Satan dreads.

I have known many days without any satanic attack; days when my mind was at peace and when things were perfectly normal and smooth in the office; when life flowed. Then suddenly, almost without warning, hundreds of things started going wrong. It is my personal opinion that demons are not assigned equally everywhere. I believe they receive assignments according to the amount of danger and threat that Satan senses.

10. You are a powerful and influential weapon against Satan. He will assign demonic forces to fragment your focus, derail your Assignment, and destroy your effectiveness. You have the potential to do great damage to Satan. You will become a special target.

11. You will be tempted a thousand times to turn back or turn away from your Assignment as were many people who followed Christ:

> *From that time many of his disciples went back, and walked no more with him.*
>
> John 6:66

12. If you want to find an excuse to turn away from the calling and anointing imparted to you, you can find a thousand exits. One minister told me, "I cannot pastor anymore because my wife does not want me to pastor." That man will stand before God to give an account of himself.

13. Do not claim to lack enough finances to complete your Assignment. God will open the book to Deuteronomy 28 and declare, "I promised you provision when you would obey My instructions." (See Deuteronomy 28:1-14.)

14. Do not blame the persecutions and criticisms received from your family members. Jesus will say:

> *And ye shall be betrayed both by parents, and brethren, and kinsfolks, and friends; and some of you shall they cause to be put to death. And ye shall be hated of all men for my name's sake. But there shall not an hair of your head perish.*
>
> Luke 21:16-18

15. Do not complain that your prayers seem to go unanswered. Jesus will reply:

> *If ye abide in me, and my words abide in you, ye shall ask what ye will, and it shall be done unto you.*
>
> John 15:7

16. Remember the reason you should complete God's Assignment for your life. Peter answered this:

> *Then Simon Peter answered him, Lord, to whom shall we go? thou hast the words of eternal life. And we believe and are sure that thou art that Christ, the Son of the living God.*
>
> John 6:68,69

17. Remember God's promise to keep alive what the Holy Spirit birthed within you:

> *Being confident of this very thing, that he which hath begun a good work in you will perform it until the day of Jesus Christ.*
>
> Philippians 1:6

18. Ask freely and often for those things which will strengthen you:

> *...Whatsoever ye shall ask the Father in my name, he will give it you. Hitherto have ye asked nothing in my name: ask, and ye shall receive, that your joy may be full.*
>
> John 16:23,24

19. Remember that God expects you to ask for wisdom continually:

> *If any of you lack wisdom, let him ask of God, that giveth to all men liberally, and upbraideth not; and it shall be given him.*
>
> James 1:5

20. Determine and forever decree that you want to complete your Assignment:

> *But let him ask in faith, nothing wavering. For he that wavereth is like a wave of the sea driven with the wind and tossed. For let not that man think that he shall receive any thing of the Lord. A double minded man is unstable in all his ways.*
>
> James 1:6-8

21. Pursue peaceful conversations instead of contentious topics:

> *Let us therefore follow after the things which make for peace, and things wherewith one may edify another.*
>
> Romans 14:19

> *But foolish and unlearned questions avoid, knowing that they do gender strifes. And the servant of the Lord must not strive; but be gentle unto all men, apt to teach, patient.*
>
> 2 Timothy 2:23,24

22. Flee the familiar traps:

> *Flee also youthful lusts....*
>
> 2 Timothy 2:22

> *For the love of money is the root of all evil: which while some coveted after, they have erred from the faith, and pierced themselves through with many sorrows. But thou, O man of God, flee these things; and follow after righteousness, godliness, faith, love, patience, meekness.*
>
> 1 Timothy 6:10,11

23. Fight tenaciously to hold on to your Assignment:

> *Fight the good fight of faith, lay hold on eternal life, whereunto thou art also called....*
>
> 1 Timothy 6:12

24. Remember Jesus. Jesus is our pattern. He is our example. He is praying and interceding to the Father for you today. The Holy Spirit is interceding for you on earth.

***Remember—endurance is your decision.***

# FACT
# 23

## YOUR ASSIGNMENT MAY BE MISUNDERSTOOD BY THOSE CLOSEST TO YOU

### WHAT BECOMES FAMILIAR OFTEN BECOMES HIDDEN

Let me explain. Suppose you have driven to your job every morning for the last five years. You see the same buildings, the same stores, and the same places of business. Then suddenly, you note something. You see a new sign or a new store.

"When did they build that?" you ask your friend!

"That has always been there," your puzzled friend replies. And it is true. That building or sign has been there for several years, but it became so familiar to you that your mind began to ignore it. It is like that with your family. You may have become so familiar to them over the years, that any new insight or direction for your Assignment may be hidden, because you are you. So here are eight insights to remember when your family does not understand your Assignment.

## 8 INSIGHTS TO HELP WHEN FRIENDS AND FAMILY MISUNDERSTAND YOU

1. What becomes familiar to the mind, the mind makes a decision to ignore. It wants something new and different. So for whatever reason, something awakened your interest.

> *Jesus tasted the bitterness of familiarity.*

Our families experience this. You have been around your brothers and sisters so long that their outstanding qualities have become familiar and are now hidden to you. Others respond and compliment them, but you do not respond to those qualities any longer because you have become accustomed to them.

2. Intellect, communication skills, and integrity do not necessarily guarantee your acceptance.

Demas, the one who forsook Paul, traveled with the apostle. How could the Gospel, communicated through the greatness and tenacity of Paul, become commonplace? But, it did. The newness and magnetism of the Gospel became too familiar:

*For Demas hath forsaken me, having loved this present world, and is departed unto Thessalonica....*

2 Timothy 4:10

3. Jesus tasted the bitterness of familiarity.

Jesus tasted loneliness and alienation from His own brothers. They became so familiar with, and accustomed to His presence, that it was difficult for them to grasp His divinity and significance:

*For neither did his brethren believe in him.*

John 7:5

4. You must stay aware that you are different from others. Jesus did:

> *Then Jesus said unto them, My time is not yet come: but your time is alway ready.*
>
> John 7:6

5. Others are not feeling your pain, your difference, or your alienation.

   You may even become the target of scorn and ridicule. Jesus' family did not understand this. Jesus knew they did not feel His pain:

> *The world cannot hate you; but me it hateth, because I testify of it, that the works thereof are evil.*
>
> John 7:7

6. Your family may be comfortable in places you are not.

   Jesus experienced this too. His brothers were comfortable in places where He was not:

> *Go ye up unto this feast: I go not up yet unto this feast; for my time is not yet full come.*
>
> John 7:8

   You too must learn to accept this. Otherwise, you may become bitter, angry, and retaliatory when those closest to you seem disloyal and disinterested:

> *But Jesus said unto them, A prophet is not without honour, but in his own country, and among his own kin, and in his own house.*
>
> Mark 6:4

I have often wished that I could have attended the "Joseph workshop." What were the great principles that enabled him to maintain his focus after his own family despised him? When he told his brothers about his remarkable dream —

■ His father *rebuked* him.
■ His brothers *envied* him.
■ He knew *rejection*.

*And he told it to his father, and to his brethren: and his father rebuked him, and said unto him, What is this dream that thou hast dreamed? Shall I and thy mother and thy brethren indeed come to bow down ourselves to thee to the earth? And his brethren envied him; but his father observed the saying.*

Genesis 37:10,11

Joseph's brothers hated his very presence. He wanted to be around them, and he sought them out. He wanted conversation and fellowship. But "when they saw him afar off, even before he came near unto them, they conspired against him to slay him" (Genesis 37:18). So what made them so angry? He was just their kid brother!

Was it his appearance? Was it his behavior and conduct? Of course not. What was their source of agitation? The answer is clearly seen in their conversation about him:

*And they said one to another, Behold, this dreamer cometh.*

Genesis 37:19

■ Joseph *had* a dream.
■ But his brothers were *intimidated* by his dreams.
■ They were *angered* by his future.
■ They were *uncomfortable* with his destiny.

■ They were *infuriated* by his goals.

■ They *misunderstood* his Assignment.

Their minds were too small for the bigness of his future. Read their words:

*Come now therefore, and let us slay him, and cast him into some pit, and we will say, Some evil beast hath devoured him....*

Genesis 37:20

■ They were willing to *scheme.*

■ They were willing to *lie.*

■ They were willing to *kill.*

It was Joseph's dreams that agitated, infuriated, and angered them. As you keep reading in Genesis 37:20, it says, "...and we shall see what become of his dreams."

■ Destiny is invisible.

■ Greatness is invisible.

Yet, its presence is so powerful that others react. The greatness and destiny of your dream cannot be refuted, doubted, or destroyed by hatred. Greatness has a presence. Destiny is like a magnet. Greatness intimidates. Destiny intimidates.

## GREATNESS ALWAYS FORCES SMALLNESS TO REACT

Look at David. He had been tending sheep. His father wanted him to bring lunch to his brothers in battle. Were they happy to see him? Were they thrilled because their young brother came to the war?

*And Eliab his eldest brother heard when he spake unto the men; and Eliab's anger was kindled against David, and he said, Why camest thou down hither? and with whom hast thou left those few sheep in the wilderness? I know thy pride, and the naughtiness of thine heart; for thou art come down that thou mightest see the battle.*

1 Samuel 17:28

What really angered his brother?

*And Eliab his eldest brother heard when he spake unto the men....*

1 Samuel 17:28

Whatever David said to the other soldiers birthed a volcano of fury within his oldest brother. David had been asking about the rewards offered to a champion of Israel who could defeat Goliath.

David was discussing the blessings, benefits and incentives for champions. He wanted something in his future more than they really did.

Your destiny lies in your real difference from others. And your difference may agitate others. It may often make others uncomfortable, miserable, and angry in your presence. But it will also determine the greatness you want to birth in your future.

7. Your family is the testing ground for the dreams and destiny God plants within You.

You cannot really run away from your family. Blood does bond. God made it so. You may experience anger, disappointment and fury. But for some unexplainable reason, you always reach back for those in your family in times of crisis, loss, or tragedy.

8. Adversity can make you more articulate.

Why? Because you are forced to explain what you feel, what you see, and what you believe in the face of those who are unbelieving. You are forced to keep yourself motivated in the presence of those who are uninspired. And you are forced to grow seeds of faith in a prevailing climate of doubt.

Those closest to you are being used of God to prepare you to become powerful on the field of battle, in the Arena of your Destiny.

So sharpen your skills. Listen closely to their observations. Consider their criticisms. God always uses time to vindicate you. Rest in that.

Sometimes those closest to you are the last to grasp what you are really about.

***Your family is your first classroom.***

# FACT
# 24

## GOD WILL NOT SHOW YOU PICTURES OF WHAT HE IS BRINGING YOU THROUGH — HE WILL SHOW YOU WHAT HE IS BRINGING YOU TO

### GOD WILL TALK TO YOU IN FAITH PICTURES

A faith picture is an imaginary picture of something that can be because of the faithfulness and promises of your heavenly Father.

Habakkuk understood "faith pictures" well: "I will stand upon my watch, and set me upon the tower, and will watch to see what he will say unto me, and what I shall answer when I am reproved" (Habakkuk 2:1).

Abraham also experienced "faith pictures." After his nephew Lot separated from him due to the strife between their employees, God spoke to Abraham, "Lift up now thine eyes, and look from the place where thou art northward, and southward, and eastward, and westward: for all the land which thou seest, to thee will I give it, and to thy seed forever" (Genesis 13:14,15).

147

Sometimes these faith pictures are created internally to hang on the walls of our imagination. And sometimes they are carefully sought out to hang on the walls of our homes. But, they are very, very important. So here are seventeen life-changing principles and keys concerning the faith pictures God will use in your life.

### 17 Life-Changing Faith Picture Principles

1. Whatever you see, you can pursue.

> Whatever you see, you can pursue.

   Mental pictures help determine your focus. Focus determines your behavior.

2. God can give you pictures of events in your future.

   He gave Abraham a faith picture of his future children:

*And I will make thy seed as the dust of the earth: so that if a man can number the dust of the earth, then shall thy seed also be numbered.*

Genesis 13:16

3. God will not always give you a picture of attacks ahead.

   God did not give Abraham a picture of his future trials and hardships. He did not give Abraham a picture of Ishmael, his son of doubt who was conceived in unbelief with Sarah's handmaid, Hagar. Neither did Abraham receive pictures in his dreams of Sodom and Gomorrah and their destruction. Nor was he given pictures of the terrible experience with Abimelech, king of Gerar. Instead, God showed Abraham pictures of his conclusion, not of his experiences en route to his goals and dreams.

4. God may talk to you in dreams.

   God showed pictures of rulership to Joseph in his night dreams:

*And he said unto them, Hear, I pray you, this dream which I have dreamed. For, behold, we were binding sheaves in the field, and, lo, my sheaf arose, and also stood upright; and, behold, your sheaves stood round about, and made obeisance to my sheaf. And his brethren said to him, Shalt thou indeed reign over us? or shalt thou indeed have dominion over us? And they hated him yet the more for his dreams, and for his words. And he dreamed yet another dream, and told it his brethren, and said, Behold, I have dreamed a dream more; and, behold, the sun and the moon and the eleven stars made obeisance to me.*

Genesis 37:6-9

5. Faith pictures inspire pursuit.

They energize us toward our dreams. And unlock the flow of faith:

*And, behold, a woman, which was diseased with an issue of blood twelve years, came behind him, and touched the hem of his garment: for she said within herself, If I may but touch his garment, I shall be whole. But Jesus turned him about, and when he saw her, he said, Daughter, be of good comfort; thy faith hath made thee whole. And the woman was made whole from that hour.*

Matthew 9:20-22

This woman had a faith picture. She saw something inside of her imagination. She honestly believed that when she could touch His garment, something would happen. And it did. This is sometimes called a point of contact.

A point of contact is anything God uses as a vehicle to inspire your faith or give it direction. A point of contact is always something that you do.

6. Your faith picture is a gift from God to unlock your faith.

When Elijah told Naaman to dip in the Jordan seven times, Naaman did so, and he was healed of leprosy. Jesus inspired a faith picture when He instructed the servants at the Cana wedding to fill the waterpots with water. The servants responded, and the water was turned into wine.

7. Pictures of prosperity unlock your faith.

Elijah used picture-power when he promised provision to the widow of Zarephath:

*...The barrel of meal shall not waste, neither shall the cruse of oil fail, until the day that the Lord sendeth rain upon the earth.*

1 Kings 17:14

8. Your faith picture strengthens you through difficult seasons.

Jesus had a picture of His victory that sustained Him. It energized Him and gave Him focus. It gave Him endurance and capability. Jesus, "...for the joy that was set before him endured the cross, despising the shame, and is set down at the right hand of the throne of God" (Hebrews 12:2).

9. Always document night dreams that inspire changes in your behavior.

Dreams can often make children suddenly interested and caring toward their parents. Perhaps they have dreams in which they see pictures involving the absence, or even the death of their parents. They motivate. They correct.

One friend of mine visits hospitals regularly. He says that seeing people in that setting motivates him to exercise, eat healthy, and take care of his body. So God can use many different methods to give you a vivid faith picture.

How important is a picture? Ask the liquor and cigarette industry. They will pay more than $780,000 for thirty seconds of pictures on a TV screen during the Super Bowl. Try to buy time on prime-time television. It would bankrupt most of us. The power of a picture cannot be overestimated.

10. Reject wrong pictures of doubt and unbelief.

Wrong pictures can grow wrong emotions and futures. Wrong pictures can make pure children impure and corrupt. They have influenced children to kill their parents while they were asleep. Wrong television programming has almost destroyed the conscience of this generation of teenagers.

11. If one wrong picture can destroy your life, then one wonderful, accurate and glorious picture of God can radically change your life forever as well.

12. The picture that dominates your mind will control your behavior.

As I pointed out when dealing with Abraham, God rarely shows you pictures of an approaching trial or a fiery furnace experience. Why? If He were to only show you pictures of an approaching trial or difficulty, you would treat the approaching adversity as a destination instead of an EXPERIENCE ALONG THE WAY.

## WHAT YOU SEE IS WHAT YOU PURSUE

So sight gives birth to desire.

Have you ever been suddenly motivated to go to the refrigerator and eat after seeing a television commercial on food? Of course you have. When you saw a commercial on physical fitness, were you inspired to join a health spa or buy a jogging suit and start walking and jogging? Certainly.

13. What you hear affects what you say to others.

Jesus Himself mentioned this about the Holy Spirit:

*...but whatsoever he shall hear, that shall he speak....*

John 16:13

## PICTURES AFFECT BEHAVIOR

14. It is crucial that you see the right pictures, and that you avoid wrong photographs of failure, defeat, and discouragement.

When Moses sent the twelve spies into Canaan in preparation for a victorious march into the promised land, ten returned with mental photographs of inferiority, failure, and unbelief:

*But the men that went up with him said, We be not able to go up against the people; for they are stronger than we. And they brought up an evil report of the land which they had searched unto the children of Israel, saying, The land, through which we have gone to search it, is a land that eateth up the inhabitants thereof; and all the people that we saw in it are men of a great stature. And there we saw the giants, the sons of Anak, which come of the giants: and we were in our own sight as grasshoppers, and so we were in their sight.*

Numbers 13:31-33

They had a picture of themselves as being inferior, weak, losers —

- They *embraced* inferiority.
- They *believed* they were too weak.
- They *spoke* defeat.

## THEY SAW GIANTS INSTEAD OF SEEING GOD

Ten of Israel's twelve spies compared themselves to the giants, instead of comparing the giants to their God. I often call what they did, *The Grasshopper Complex. The Grasshopper Complex* defeats you from the inside. Enemies are really unnecessary, since you choose to become your own worst enemy when you allow *The Grasshopper Complex* to grow within you.

The Israelites did not forfeit Canaan because of giants. They lost Canaan because of doubt, unbelief, and nurturing wrong photographs of themselves. They studied their difference in physical strength instead of in spiritual power.

But Joshua and Caleb nurtured a photograph of their victories. They chose to believe in the power of God instead of the strength of their opposition.

You must do the same to achieve the great things God wants you to achieve.

Every child has painful memories. Sometimes, there is a memory of a father who screamed out, "You are so stupid. You will never amount to anything. You are nothing but a bum!" The mental photograph finds a landing place in a child's imagination. Then an exasperated mother blurts out, "I wish I never had any of you children. It was a mistake to have you!" The photograph produced from believing such a thing reinforces and strengthens as time goes on.

■ Wrong photographs *destroy* good people.

■ Faith pictures can *correct* damaged people.

15. You will experience the greatest faith pictures of your life when you spend time in *The Secret Place.*

When you spend time in *The Secret Place,* wrong pictures die, and RIGHT pictures come alive — in His presence.

Then, when someone steps into your life and announces, "I have a word from the Lord for you," you will be able to judge it spiritually. God rarely gives you photographs of what He is bringing you through, but encourages you with a picture of His desired end:

> *For I know the thoughts that I think toward you, saith the Lord, thoughts of peace, and not of evil, to give you an expected end.*
>
> Jeremiah 29:11

16. When a true prophet has a word from God for you, the faith picture will bring peace.

So pay attention to faith pictures. Noah's ark was a prophetic picture of the ark of God's safety through Jesus. The tabernacle of Israel was a photograph of God's plan of redemption through the blood of Christ. The union of wife and husband is a photograph of the body of Christ linked to Jesus, our Head.

17. What you keep seeing affects what you keep doing:

> *The light of the body is the eye: if therefore thine eye be single, thy whole body shall be full of light. But if thine eye be evil, thy whole body shall be full of darkness. If therefore the light that is in thee be darkness, how great is that darkness!*
>
> Matthew 6:22,23

*Faith pictures from the Holy Spirit will generate faith. Everything you do after you receive a faith picture will be a subconscious attempt to make your faith picture come true.*

# FACT
## 25

## Any Satanic Attack Reveals What Satan Fears Most in Your Future

### Your Past Is Over
### Your Future Is Feared

Think about your mind for a moment. Your mind has two functions — the memory and the imagination. The purpose of your memory is to replay events in your past. The purpose of your imagination is to preplay events in your future.

Now, your past is over, and Satan has no fear of it. He merely uses it as a memory to taunt, intimidate, and demoralize you. But it is over. God does not remember the sin in your past. So why should you?

*For as the heaven is high above the earth, so great is his mercy toward them that fear him. As far as the east is from the west, so far hath he removed our transgressions from us.*
Psalm 103:11,12

155

Years ago, Satan kept replaying a moment of disappointment in my life. He played it over and over again. Exasperated, I asked the Lord, "Why does Satan keep doing this?"

"He is running low on material!" was the inner impression from the Holy Spirit.

> When Satan keeps showing you the same photographs of yesterday's failures, it is only an indication that he is "running low on material."

So when Satan keeps showing you the same photographs of yesterday's failures, it is only an indication that he is "running low on material." He has nothing fresh to flash on the screen of your mind. He is simply scrambling to find worthless old photographs to paralyze you emotionally and spiritually.

It is important for you to move quickly away from the memories that destroy you:

*Remember ye not the former things, neither consider the things of old.*
Isaiah 43:18

Focusing on tomorrow moves you away from yesterday:

*Behold, I will do a new thing; now it shall spring forth; shall ye not know it? I will even make a way in the wilderness, and rivers in the desert.*
Isaiah 43:19

Your future is intimidating to Satan. Look at the life of Moses. What stirred Pharaoh to kill the newborn Hebrews? The Hebrews were his slaves. But somehow, in the spirit world, an awareness emerged that a champion was in the womb of a woman of God. That coming champion would lead the exodus of the Israelites out of Egypt. And Pharaoh was about to lose millions of slaves who labored for him. So Pharaoh's attack on the children revealed the potential of those children and was a threat to Satan. It would be devastating to his demonic rule.

Remember, the deliverer had been promised as Satan stood listening in Genesis 3:15:

*And I will put enmity between thee and the woman, and between thy seed and her seed; it shall bruise thy head, and thou shalt bruise his heel.*

And what about Herod? What caused him to suddenly kill all the children two years old and under? He:

*...slew all the children that were in Bethlehem, and in all the coasts thereof, from two years old and under....*
                                                                Matthew 2:16

The king's authority was threatened because some mother's child would carry a greater authority that would displace him from his throne.

I have been intrigued about just this sort of phenomenon for many years. When some minister who has been greatly used in healing shares his testimony, it seems inevitable that he suffered through some incurable or severe childhood disease. As it was with Moses and Jesus, Satan tried to kill them before God could bring their deliverance about.

Remember, wherever you fight your greatest battle is where you experience your greatest victories and triumphs. And the photograph of your triumph is in the pain of your trial. If you look long enough at your trial, you will see the photograph of your promotion emerge clearly for your spirit to discern.

So listen carefully to those whom God is using to bring healing in marriages and broken relationships. Almost every one of them has known abuse, rejection, or some deep sorrowful experience of a broken childhood home.

And take some time to review the nature of the attacks you have experienced repeatedly. Ask the Holy Spirit to reveal the path He is qualifying and assigning for your walk. Someone has well said, "The pain you can feel is the pain you can heal."

*Your tears of TODAY will be the rain on someone's desert TOMORROW.*

## FACT 26

### YOUR ASSIGNMENT WILL REQUIRE SEASONS OF PRAYERFUL ISOLATION

#### IT IS NATURAL TO DESIRE THE PRESENCE OF OTHERS

There will be moments in the pursuit of your Assignment when you feel totally alienated from those you love. It will appear as if they do not understand. It will seem that you alone are motivated to complete the instructions for your own life.

Jesus may have felt this way immediately following His baptism:

*Then was Jesus led up of the Spirit into the wilderness to be tempted of the devil. And when he had fasted forty days and forty nights, he was afterward and hungered.*

Matthew 4:1,2

#### THE TEMPTER TIMES HIS TEMPTATIONS

Satan does not attend baptisms. At Jesus' baptism, the crowd was there. The motivation was there. The currents of joy were like a flurry of bright clouds around Him. So Satan waited until Jesus was alone and isolated from the encouragement of others. Then he approached.

In fact, almost every major satanic attack will occur when you are alone.

> When you are listening only to others, you may not hear God talk.

So why does God permit you to be alone? Because those are the moments when He reveals His presence, His purpose, His plan, and His power. When you are listening only to others, you may not hear God talk. So isolation is more than emotional emptiness. It provokes absolute dependence upon the Holy Spirit. It is during these times that you develop an addiction to His presence, which is the only true proof of maturity.

When David was isolated and separated from his family while tending sheep, God gave him victories nobody else observed:

*And David said unto Saul, Thy servant kept his father's sheep, and there came a lion, and a bear, and took a lamb out of the flock: and I went out after him, and smote him, and delivered it out of his mouth: and when he arose against me, I caught him by his beard, and smote him, and slew him. Thy servant slew both the lion and the bear....*

1 Samuel 17:34-36

- Ministers *feel isolated* when their message is misunderstood and not embraced.

- Mothers *feel isolated* when a father will not stand behind them in their instruction to the children.

- Fathers *feel isolated* when their labors are ignored and unappreciated.

- Employees *feel isolated* when only their mistakes are acknowledged.
- Children *feel isolated* when parents are too busy to stop and focus on their conversations.
- Husbands *feel isolated* when their wives show more excitement over their children than they show toward them.
- Wives *feel isolated* when husbands would rather work overtime than be with their family.

I have known many times of isolation throughout my fifty years of living. There have been times when I made the mistake of searching out a substitute for His presence. Perhaps I would sit down and watch television to distract and break my focus off the emptiness within me. Sometimes I have reached for the telephone to call a friend.

The most important thing you can do during your moments of isolation is to reach for the One who is awaiting you. He wants to be pursued. He craves relationship:

*Call unto me, and I will answer thee, and shew thee great and mighty things, which thou knowest not.*

Jeremiah 33:3

You are on His mind:

*For I know the thoughts that I think toward you, saith the Lord, thoughts of peace, and not of evil, to give you an expected end. Then shall ye call upon me, and ye shall go and pray unto me, and I will hearken unto you. And ye shall seek me, and find me, when ye shall search for me with all your heart.*

Jeremiah 29:11-13

You will find Him during times of isolation:

> *And I will be found of you, saith the Lord: and I will turn away your captivity....*
>
> Jeremiah 29:14

Seasons of isolation pass. But they are important in revealing the limitations of our loved ones. These seasons reveal the deep need we have for God. They also fuel and nurture continuous focus on Him for our Assignment.

- Private victories can *birth* public victories.
- Private victories can *lead* to public honor.
- These times *build* character.
- These times also birth *revelation* of the power of God.

**But most importantly, these times of vulnerability can create an obsession with His presence.**

# FACT
# 27

## YOUR ASSIGNMENT MAY SOMETIMES SEEM TO BE IN VAIN

### GREAT EFFORTS DO NOT ALWAYS PRODUCE IMMEDIATE RESULTS

Harvest takes time. Any farmer knows this. He arises early in the morning to sow his seed. Rains come. The sun beats down. There are hours of toil and days of waiting. Then, the small plants begin to bud, and changes occur day after day. Suddenly, it appears his entire land is filled with a bountiful crop. But the blessing came after days of toil, sweat, hard labor, time, and money invested — after a season of waiting...waiting...and more waiting.

The apostle Paul felt this way when he wrote, "I am afraid of you, lest I have bestowed upon you labour in vain" (Galatians 4:11). He had poured his life out. He had spoken courageously, eloquently, and consistently. Yet, he felt useless at times.

### WAITING FOR CHANGE IS PROOF OF YOUR FAITH

This is the kind of faith that moves the hand of God toward your life. I remember when I first grasped that a mantle of wisdom was upon my life. It was not my possession of wisdom, but my pursuit of it that revealed my calling. I had an obsession to know the heart and mind of God toward a matter. When I shared this with a preacher friend of mine, he laughingly replied, "Nobody wants wisdom, Mike! Everybody wants miracles!"

*Most of us want changes without the seasons of change.*

Well, I watched it happen before my eyes. Nobody seemed to desire wisdom. Everybody wanted an immediate turnaround miracle touch from God. They would sit for three hours in a service anticipating a miracle, but would not invest in a wisdom book. Most of us want changes without the seasons of change.

Ministers often feel useless. They lose confidence in people. The prophet Micah often felt that his Assignment was in vain. Listen to his assessment of those to whom he was assigned: "The best of them is as a brier: the most upright is sharper than a thorn hedge...Trust ye not in a friend..." (Micah 7:4,5). Have you ever felt that way? Of course you have. I have too.

The great king and musician David once sobbed, "Why art thou cast down, O my soul? and why art thou disquieted within me?" (Psalm 42:11). Yes, the same brave and courageous lad who ran toward Goliath with a slingshot also knew the experience of feeling like his labors were futile.

Jeremiah considered managing a "motel" in the desert rather than staying in the ministry:

> *Oh that I had in the wilderness a lodging place of wayfaring men; that I might leave my people, and go from them!...*

Jeremiah 9:2

Elijah, who could outrun horses and call down fire on water-soaked sacrifices, once hit total despondency and begged God to kill him:

> *But he himself went a day's journey into the wilderness, and came and sat down under a juniper tree: and he requested for himself that he might die; and said, It is enough; now, O Lord, take away my life; for I am not better than my fathers.*
>
> 1 Kings 19:4

Jesus, also, must have felt at times that His labors were in vain. Once while in the middle of explaining some powerful truths to His disciples, Peter, His own disciple, rebuked Him. So Jesus had to turn and say, "Get thee behind me, Satan: thou art an offense unto me: for thou savourest not the things that be of God, but those that be of men" (Matthew 16:23). Imagine having one of the closest prayer partners in your life misunderstand almost everything you say. One day Jesus finally cried out, "O faithless and perverse generation, how long shall I be with you? How long shall I suffer you?" (Matthew 17:17.)

- ■ Seasons change.
- ■ People change.
- ■ Your own needs and desires will change.

So let patience do its work:

> *Cast not away therefore your confidence, which hath great recompence of reward. For ye have need of patience, that, after ye have done the will of God, ye might receive the promise.*
>
> Hebrews 10:35,36

*And never, never, never give up — because your future will always whimper at the feet of persistence.*

## YOUR ASSIGNMENT MAY REQUIRE UNUSUAL AND UNWAVERING TRUST IN A MAN OR WOMAN OF GOD

### YOU WILL HAVE TO TRUST SOMEBODY

It is true that you cannot trust everyone. You certainly cannot trust everyone every day of your life. But when God determines to bless you, He will place someone close to you with an instruction, an encouragement, or a warning that will greatly influence your life. And when they speak, it will be your willingness to trust their word from God that could be the difference between total failure or remarkable success in your life.

But submitting is not always easy. Why? Because the person you are trusting is deciding your future.

Let me explain: God uses a chain of authority continuously in your life. That is why the apostle Paul encouraged children to obey their parents, employees to honor their boss, and Christians to honor the man of God in their lives.

One of the most powerful principles in Scripture, hidden like a nugget of gold, is:

*...Believe in the Lord your God, so shall ye be established; believe his prophets, so shall ye prosper.*

2 Chronicles 20:20

## DOUBT IS COSTLY

Skepticism has created the greatest losses on earth. Unbelief creates disasters as quickly as faith produces miracles. Millions of sinners have forfeited an incredible life in Christ because they refused to trust in the words of a man of God. To many, the preaching of the Gospel is foolishness:

Doubt is costly.

*For the preaching of the cross is to them that perish foolishness; but unto us which are saved it is the power of God...it pleased God by the foolishness of preaching to save them that believe.*

1 Corinthians 1:18,21

## GOD OFTEN PACKAGES HIS GOLD IN BURLAP BAGS

You see, the man that God chooses to use may not be intellectual, articulate, or skilled. He may even be naive, uneducated, and uncouth. John the Baptist was certainly not pleasing in appearance by modern standards. But those who embraced his word from God were ushered into new levels of power and were changed forever.

The apostle Paul did not impress everyone. He acknowledged this when he wrote the church in Corinth:

*And I, brethren, when I came to you, came not with excellency of speech or of wisdom, declaring unto you the testimony of God...And I was with you in weakness, and in fear, and in much trembling. And my speech and my preaching was not with enticing words of man's wisdom, but in demonstration of the Spirit and of power: that your faith should not stand in the wisdom of men, but in the power of God.*

1 Corinthians 2:1,3-5

Your financial breakthrough may depend on your willingness to believe a man of God. Your financial provision may require total obedience to the instruction from a man of God. It happened to the widow of Zarephath. She was emaciated and broken, her son was starving, and she was down to her last meal. Then one day, the prophet Elijah knocked on the door of her home with a bold and almost incredulous instruction. The instruction: she was to give him a meal even before she and her son ate.

You see, the instruction of a man of God will rarely be logical. You can do the logical thing without a man of God in your life. But you will rarely do an illogical act unless a man of God stirs your faith. Somewhere, at some time, you will need a man of God to move you from the pit of logic to the palace of faith. Elijah did it:

*And Elijah said unto her, Fear not; go and do as thou hast said: but make me thereof a little cake first, and bring it unto me, and after make for thee and for thy son. For thus saith the Lord God of Israel, The barrel of meal shall not waste, neither shall the cruse of oil fail, until the day that the Lord sendeth rain upon the earth.*

1 Kings 17:13,14

## YOUR REACTION TO A MAN OF GOD DETERMINES GOD'S REACTION TO YOU

This is so important: when a man of God gives you an instruction, there is a judgment or a reward that your obedience will produce. If he is a true man of God:

- He *will not* give you an instruction to demonstrate his authority.
- He *will not* give you an instruction to merely finance his own dreams.
- His instruction *will* be an exit from your present crisis.
- And his instruction *will* provide your entry into God's miracle harvest.

## YOUR OBEDIENCE WILL DETERMINE YOUR OWN REWARD

The widow in Zarephath obeyed. Her account proved that the golden key to success always involves obedience to an instruction from God:

> *And she went and did according to the saying of Elijah: and she, and he, and her house, did eat many days. And the barrel of meal wasted not, neither did the cruse of oil fail, according to the word of the Lord, WHICH HE SPAKE BY ELIJAH.*
>
> 1 Kings 17:15,16

Read 1 Kings 17 carefully and you will not find a single verse that indicates the widow recognized or heard the voice of God directly. It was the prophet who heard God, and she heard the prophet.

- *God* spoke to the prophet.
- The *prophet* spoke to the widow.

■ This sequence is honored by God.

So when man refuses to accept an instruction through someone God sends, he loses every promise and reward God had intended.

When God wants to bless you, He may talk to a man of God about your life. When God wants to stop judgment, He will usually send a man of God with a warning. He did so for Nineveh:

*Now the word of the Lord came unto Jonah the son of Amittai, saying, arise, go to Nineveh, that great city, and cry against it; for their wickedness is come up before me.*

Jonah 1:1,2

Now, Jonah was disobedient. And his experience in "Seaweed University" is known around the world. His disobedience was costly — he was swallowed by a fish. So when he finally arrived in Nineveh, he was a persuaded man.

## PERSUADED MEN PERSUADE

Let me say this: thousands of people have no idea what a man of God experiences prior to giving an instruction to someone. There have been many times in my life when an instruction came from the Lord in the night for people, when actually, I did not want to do it because it was not always encouraging. I have been given instructions of judgment more than once. But the reason I obeyed was not to secure the approval, applause, or acceptance of people. I obeyed because I had a powerful God speaking powerfully and persuasively into my ear. My disobedience would be too costly.

Jonah cried in the streets of Nineveh, "...Yet forty days, and Nineveh shall be overthrown" (Jonah 3:4). Somehow, the credibility and truth of Jonah's message was felt, and the people were repentant:

> *So the people of Nineveh believed God, and proclaimed a fast, and put on sackcloth, from the greatest of them even to the least of them. For word came unto the king of Nineveh, and he arose from his throne, and he laid his robe from him, and covered him with sackcloth, and sat in ashes. And he caused it to be proclaimed and published through Nineveh by the decree of the king and his nobles, saying, Let neither man nor beast, herd nor flock, taste any thing: let them not feed, nor drink water: but let man and beast be covered with sackcloth, and cry mightily unto God: yea, let them turn every one from his evil way, and from the violence that is in their hands. Who can tell if God will turn and repent, and turn away from his fierce anger, that we perish not?*
>
> Jonah 3:5-9

Think about this; the king wept and cried. The people were instructed to stop feeding their animals, and the people and government leaders of Nineveh went without food.

So something supernatural happens when you decide to believe a man of God. What was Nineveh's reward for trusting the word of a man of God?

> *And God saw their works, that they turned from their evil way; and God repented of the evil, that he had said that he would do unto them; and he did it not.*
>
> Jonah 3:10

I recently had a very unusual experience that changed my life. Each year I host a World Wisdom Conference. Two years ago at this conference, one of my friends, a visiting evangelist, came to me saying, "I feel that God spoke to me to receive an offering for your ministry today."

To this I replied, "Well, I will let you know whatever God impresses me to do." I appreciated what he said, but really felt that I was able to hear from God as much as anyone present. And I felt no leading whatsoever that an offering was to be received at that time.

Then a few minutes later, another evangelist handed me a note. It reiterated what the other brother felt impressed to share about receiving an offering. They both felt it was God and wanted me to hand him the microphone.

I was agitated. I had a personal schedule for the time that offerings would be received and my basic attitude was, "This is my own conference, and nobody is going to receive an offering unless I approve and know that it is God's will. This is neither the time nor the place for an offering." I had already received an offering that morning, and I did not want the people to feel harassed.

I am not a novice in the ministry. I have walked to the pulpit more than twelve thousand times since I started preaching at the age of eight years old. I spoke at my first crusade when I was fifteen. I entered full-time evangelism at the age of nineteen. Since then I have been in thirty-six countries of the world. So I was a little peeved that another man of God would push me in this manner.

Now, while I was speaking and preparing to dismiss the people for lunch, this same evangelist walked up to me publicly. He was weeping and crying. "Brother, could I say a word?"

I was still frustrated. It bothered me deeply. I pray, fast, and make every effort to hear the voice of the Holy Spirit. And I was hearing nothing from God. I felt nothing and really believed in my heart that he was totally out of order.

But he was a man of God. I knew he was a man of God. His ministry was proven. His anointing was obvious. He had passed the test of time. He wore the badge of endurance. He was gentle and kind, but very persistent. So I reluctantly handed him the microphone.

As he began to speak, tears ran down his cheeks. Then within moments, my partners began to step out of their seats streaming to the front with $1,000 faith promises for the ministry. They kept coming, and coming, and coming. I stood there, still feeling nothing. I could hardly believe what was happening. I cannot say that I felt joy, because I did not feel joy. Neither did I feel any confirmation. During the entire time that he received the offering, I never felt the winds of the Holy Spirit, and the offering that day in cash and pledges totaled more than $100,000.

So I prayed, "Oh Lord, I thought I knew Your voice. I thought I knew when You spoke."

But you see, God had spoken something. He had spoken to another man something that He had withheld from me. And it concerned me deeply. In fact, I was incensed. I was embarrassed. I was puzzled. I am sure that was the way Eli the priest felt when God spoke to Samuel, the little boy, instead of to him, the high priest.

I felt the timing was wrong. I had my own schedule. The only reason I had finally allowed and permitted him to do what he did was because I really knew he was a man of God. The touch of God was upon him while I felt nothing. I saw no vision and experienced no revelation as I simply trusted in the man of God that my Father had decided to use that day.

The whole thing continues to irritate me, but I learned a valuable lesson that day.

I learned that God tells others things He will not tell me. And I learned that my success can depend on my ability to recognize a man of God when I am in his presence.

Once when I was ministering on the East coast, a remarkable anointing came upon me as I started sharing a personal testimony regarding the planting of a $58 seed. I told the congregation:

"Six years ago I was sitting on the platform in Washington, D.C., while the pastor was receiving the tithes and offerings. I had been sowing a seed of $1,000 each month into that church for the previous twelve months.

"Then while the pastor was receiving the tithes, the Holy Spirit suddenly spoke to me by asking this question. 'How many kinds of blessings are in My Word?' He asked.

"I had done a private study, and in my research, I had found fifty-eight different kinds of blessings. Now, there may be more depending on your own selection of categories, but that is what I counted. So I replied, 'There are fifty-eight different kinds of blessings in Your Word.'

"So He said, 'I want you to plant a special seed of $58 in this offering. Write Covenant of Blessing on the check." And He told me that He wanted this seed of $58 to represent a covenant of blessing between Him and me. I thought it was ridiculous. But as I listened from my heart, I knew it was His voice, so I obeyed.

"A few moments later, the Holy Spirit instructed me to plant another seed for someone I loved who needed a miracle in their life. I obeyed. And within weeks, miracles occurred in my life that were explosive and life-changing."

This is what I shared in that Sunday morning service. And as a result, I explained to the people that I felt strongly impressed that each person present should also sow a seed of $58 toward the work of the Lord. I told them it would be used to purchase television time to teach the Gospel. Many obeyed that instruction — not because they heard the voice of God, but because they believed that a man of God was giving them an appropriate and godly instruction.

Later that afternoon, one of the men visiting the church called the pastor. He was irate. He was an ungodly man who did not follow the Lord and he told the pastor that the whole thing was a scheme, a hoax, a trap. You see, when you do not know God, it is obvious that you will not necessarily recognize a man of God. When you live in daily disobedience, it is normal to continue in that disobedience when an instruction comes from God.

But in that same service, another visiting pastor took her checkbook and planted a $58 seed. She believed that the mantle of favor would be wrapped around her life because she obeyed an instruction I had given.

A few months later, an elderly man she had ministered to died, and left this lady pastor a church paid for in full, two homes, and twenty-seven acres of land. The blessings of God exploded in her life because she had obeyed the instructions of a man of God. They were not logical. They were beyond human comprehension. She did not "buy a miracle." She had simply obeyed an instruction.

- ■ The man who *criticized*...lost his harvest.
- ■ The woman who *obeyed*...created a harvest.

Two people in the same service produced two different results. Oh, please hear me today! When God wants to bless you, He will anoint a wonderful man or woman of God to give you an instruction. It may be illogical. It may even seem ridiculous. But do you remember a man by the name of Naaman? He had leprosy. He was the captain of the host of the armies of Syria. Yet when he willingly obeyed the instruction of a prophet to dip in the Jordan River seven times, his leprosy disappeared.

It will happen the same way in your life. When you know someone is truly a man or woman of God, be swift to embrace their instruction.

*Your destiny is your decision.*

## FACT
## 29

# YOU ARE THE ONLY ONE
# GOD HAS ANOINTED FOR
# YOUR SPECIFIC ASSIGNMENT

## YOUR ASSIGNMENT REQUIRES
## YOUR PARTICIPATION

Nobody else can discern it for you. Nobody else can pursue it for you. Nobody else can complete it for you:

*So then every one of us shall give account of himself to God.*

Romans 14:12

It is sad to listen to those who blame their circumstances on others. I have often listened to a husband whine, "I want to do it, but my wife does not agree with me." Wives often complain, "My husband will not cooperate with my calling and Assignment."

So stop blaming others for your personal decisions. One of the most important principles spoken into my life by the Holy Spirit has been the Wisdom Key: NEVER COMPLAIN ABOUT WHAT YOU PERMIT.

## INTOLERANCE OF YOUR PRESENT SITUATION WILL CREATE A DIFFICULT FUTURE

Never forget that your present circumstances in life are existing with your permission. And that your toleration of them breathes life and longevity into them. But also understand that intolerance of your present situation will create a different future. And that nothing will really change in your life until you cannot tolerate it any longer.

*Stop blaming others for your personal decisions.*

The apostle Paul was very direct about the matter when he said: "But let every man prove his own work, and then shall he have rejoicing in himself alone, and not in another" (Galatians 6:4). You see, God never intended for you to depend on everyone else for the completion of your Assignment. Your real joy will always be dependent upon His presence. His presence is dependent upon your pursuit. And your pursuit will always be your own decision.

Certainly, hindrances do occur. It is common to have relationships that slow us down, demotivate, and discourage us. Every achiever has experienced a connection with someone who was a burden instead of a blessing. But you have chosen your friendships! And the quality of the relationships that you have chosen reflects and reveals what you respect the most in life. When I read the biographies of extraordinary champions, they continuously take personal responsibility for their own actions, decisions, and the tasks necessary to reach their goals and dreams.

"I really hate my job," one man confessed to me.

"Then, why are you staying there?" I asked, quite puzzled.

"It is close to my house," was his ridiculous reply.

Again, never forget that it is you who have chosen the present. And it is you who can keep it or change it. You may complain, whine, and gripe for the rest of your life. But you have chosen the environment surrounding you. You have accepted it. You have embraced it. You have refused to walk away from it. So stop finding fault with it.

## YOUR PRESENT EXISTS WITH YOUR PERMISSION

The apostle Paul took personal responsibility for his life. Then at the close of it, he wrote Timothy, "I have fought a good fight, I have finished my course, I have kept the faith" ( 2 Timothy 4:7).

Nobody else could fight his fight. Nobody else could finish his course. Nobody else could run his race. Only Paul could keep his faith. And only Paul could keep his focus. So he fought his own fight.

You must grasp this. You must decide the conclusion of your life that you desire. You must decide to run your own race. You must grow the kind of harvest you desire. Like Paul, you must pursue the relationships that matter to you, not to others:

> *Wherefore, my beloved, as ye have always obeyed, not as in my presence only, but now much more in my absence, work out your own salvation with fear and trembling.*
> Philippians 2:12

This is why your complaining must stop. You are responsible for your situations. "Do all things without murmurings and disputings" Paul also says (Philippians 2:14).

Jesus, our example and pattern, declared, "...I have finished the work which thou gavest me to do" (John 17:4). When saying this, He took responsibility for his own Assignment.

Are you deeply disturbed and uncomfortable with your life right now? If you are, here are four keys that can move you from discomfort into the proper season of your Assignment.

## 4 ASSIGNMENT "CHECK-UP" KEYS

1. First, ask yourself probing, sincere, and direct questions.

   ■ Have you exhausted the benefits of your present season?

   ■ Have you extracted from your boss or mentors everything they have wanted to pour into you?

   ■ Does your present schedule reveal that you have honored your priorities in the eyes of God?

   ■ Have you excelled and given your very best to those you are laboring among at this time?

You see, if you have not emptied and maximized your life into the present, you are unqualified to enter your future. Your future is a reward, not a guarantee. This is why the apostle Paul wrote the following statement after discussing the quality of his fight and the finishing of his course:

> *Henceforth there is laid up for me a crown of righteousness, which the Lord, the righteous judge, shall give me at that day: and not me only, but unto all them that love his appearing.*
>
> 2 Timothy 4:8

2. Second, have you spent enough time in His presence to hear the voice of the Holy Spirit? You see, He is your Mentor and Advisor. And if He is not speaking into your life daily and observing your continuous acts of obedience, nothing in your life could possibly be accurate. Consequently, your personal assessments of your life may be distorted and inaccurate.

3. Third, are you living in rebellion to any known law of God? I have found that it is impossible to experience total peace when one moment of my daily life is lived in opposition to His laws:

> *And whatsoever we ask, we receive of him, because we keep his commandments, and do those things that are pleasing in his sight.*
>
> 1 John 3:22

4. And fourth, ask yourself, is the future I am desiring worth my seed of patience and the investment of preparation?

Moses wanted to be the deliverer for Israel. But he had to endure seasons of preparation. Jesus had thirty years of preparation before His public ministry. There have been times in my own life when I have deeply desired a different future, but was unwilling to pay the price of preparation for it.

Your Assignment is something you do, not something you observe. Read the writings of the apostle Paul when he says, " I follow after... I do... I press... I beseech... I entreat thee...." (See Philippians 3:12-4:3.)

*Your Assignment will require your own personal choices and appropriate actions. It will require your personal achievements, productivity, accomplishments, and energy.*

# FACT
# 30

## YOU MUST ONLY ATTEMPT A GOD-GIVEN AND GOD-APPROVED ASSIGNMENT

### GOD WILL NEVER SUSTAIN WHAT HE HAS NOT BIRTHED

"I am leaving the evangelistic field and birthing a new church," said a young minister several months ago.

"So God has commanded you to become a pastor?" I asked.

"Not really," he replied, "but my wife is tired of my traveling. I have two children that I need to raise. It is the only thing I can do right now."

"You are going to birth a church without the command and instruction of the Holy Spirit?" I asked incredulously.

At that, he hung his head, and stared ahead for a few moments. He could not answer. He could not defend his idea.

We have become so accustomed to creating and designing our own blueprints for life these days, that we often only consult the Holy Spirit in crisis situations. But it is quite possible that the crisis would not arrive at all had He been consulted first. Ideas, such as this young minister's are only options. But when God speaks, He gives instructions which are not to be altered, ignored, or refuted.

*God will never sustain what He has not birthed.*

You will often hear someone talk about a "God-idea." Obviously, this is intended to convey the thought that God would inspire an invention or a new method for doing something. It is based on Proverbs 8:12: "I wisdom dwell with prudence, and find out knowledge of witty inventions." Yes, God inspires many wonderful improvements and corrections in our lives. But in reality, a thought or idea is not necessarily a command.

If you study the Bible carefully, there is no record in Scripture of where God gave anyone an idea. Rather, He gives instructions. He gives commands.

There were occasions in Scripture when someone sinned, and God let them choose the type of judgment they could experience. It happened in the life of David, after his sin. When he numbered Israel, it displeased the Lord:

> *And David said unto God, I have sinned greatly, because I have done this thing: but now, I beseech thee, do away the iniquity of thy servant; for I have done very foolishly.*

> 1 Chronicles 21:8

When God spoke to the prophet Gad, He told Gad to "Go and tell David, saying, Thus saith the Lord, I offer thee three things: choose thee one of them, that I may do it unto thee" (1 Chronicles 21:10). David replied, "...let me fall now into the hand of the Lord; for very great are his mercies: but let me not fall into the hand of man" (1 Chronicles 21:13).

The message of David's "numbering" episode, is that it is crucial that you do not attempt to achieve a dream or a goal that God has not instructed you to pursue. Wrong goals can become substitutes for right goals. Wrong dreams can become substitutes for the right dreams. And when you pursue something God did not intend you to have, He is not obligated to sustain you emotionally, physically, or financially.

## ANYTHING YOU PURSUE ALONE WILL FAIL

One day after David had conquered his enemies, he was sitting in his house when he indicated to Nathan the prophet that he wanted to build a special house for God. The prophet immediately responded, "Go, do all that is in thine heart; for the Lord is with thee" (2 Samuel 7:3).

But even prophets can be wrong when they fail to consult God. So that evening God spoke to Nathan to bring a special word to David. The word was that David was not to build the house of the Lord and that his seed would do so instead:

> *...I will set up thy seed after thee, which shall proceed out of thy bowels, and I will establish his kingdom. He shall build an house for my name....*
>
> 2 Samuel 7:12,13

Mentors often see the future of their protégés years in advance. Solomon was David's seed who would eventually build the temple:

> *And Solomon sent to Hiram, saying, Thou knowest how that David my father could not build an house unto the name of the Lord his God for the wars which were about him on every side, until the Lord put them under the soles of his feet. But now the Lord my God hath given me rest on every side,*

*so that there is neither adversary nor evil occurrent. And, behold, I purpose to build an house unto the name of the Lord my God, as the Lord spake unto David my father, saying, Thy son, whom I will set upon thy throne in thy room, he shall build an house unto my name.*

1 Kings 5:2-5

You will have many wonderful and inspired ideas throughout your lifetime. But again, an idea is not a command from God. When God is involved, it will not be simply an idea: it will be an instruction and command.

I have pursued several projects throughout my lifetime that God did not put His hand upon. They exhausted me emotionally, physically, spiritually, and financially. Looking back across the pages of my achievements now, I truly wish that I had waited for a direct command from the Holy Spirit on each project.

Why do we pursue wrong projects? For several reasons. I recently talked to a minister who had invested millions of dollars into a hotel. His congregation and partners had urged him to do so in order to have convenient access to his ministry and services. But God did not instruct him to do so. The needs of the people motivated him instead of the voice of the Holy Spirit. And he paid dearly through some tragic situations that resulted because of it.

It is easy to be stirred and motivated by the needs of those close to you instead of by the voice of God. When it happens, you can bring disasters and heartache into your life. So the needs of others are not necessarily commands from God.

Sometimes, our own boredom with the same routine inspires us to try something different. One of the greatest evangelists in our generation once told me, "Mike, the biggest mistake of my life was when I got tired of doing the same thing over and over again. I decided I wanted to see something change, and that was the biggest mistake of my ministry. I lost hundreds of thousands of partners and support. I simply missed God," he said.

One of my great mentors once told me, "When you get sick and tired of saying something, you are just then beginning to get it yourself. When your staff gets sick and tired of hearing you say something, they are just then beginning to get it. And when your people get sick and tired of hearing you teach something, they are just then beginning to understand it."

So fight against boredom by returning to His presence for fresh inspiration and any new instructions. Do not permit your imagination to become your guide in scheduling your Assignment.

When I have invested time in *The Secret Place* to receive confirmation and reassurance concerning the will of God, His inner peace has sustained me in crises and the difficult times that occur; knowing that "...If God be for us, who can be against us?" (Romans 8:31.)

## ANY WORTHWHILE ASSIGNMENT CREATES ENEMIES

So it is vital that you know beyond any doubt that God will be an enemy to your enemies, a friend to your friends, and will walk with you through the completion of any instruction.

Another reason we attempt projects that God did not inspire is salesmanship. Someone who is articulate and persuasive convinces us that something is the "chance of a lifetime." And that we had better do it now, or it will be our last opportunity forever. But nothing is more plentiful than opportunities. The universe is crammed with millions of them.

You will never lack for an opportunity. It is your ability to focus and give your best effort to any opportunity that makes the difference. So ask yourself this, "How much influence has God had in my past decisions? How much private time have I invested in *The Secret Place* regarding a project?

When I stay in *The Secret Place* (my private prayer room dedicated to the Holy Spirit), my conclusions are always different from those of advisors. Why? Because God sees further ahead than anyone. He is swift to convey His answers when pursued.

> *Except the Lord build the house, they labour in vain that build it....*
>
> Psalm 127:1

I believe it. So keep listening for the voice of the Holy Spirit. He will speak when His opinion is respected, treasured, and pursued.

***Nobody else is responsible for your Assignment but you.***

**FACT**
**31**

## YOUR ASSIGNMENT WILL SUCCEED BECAUSE OF SOMETHING GOD HAS CHOSEN TO ANOINT IN YOUR LIFE

### YOUR ASSIGNMENT'S SUCCESS WILL DEPEND ON THE ANOINTING

I cannot emphasize this enough. The anointing is a specific enabling from the Holy Spirit to solve an immediate problem. He imparts power to remove burdens and destroy yokes. It is the power of God to correct.

So here are eighteen keys to help you keep the anointing vibrant and alive in your life.

### 18 KEYS TO UNDERSTANDING THE ANOINTING

1. You have been given something God can use. Find it:

> *But the manifestation of the Spirit is given to every man to profit withal.*
>
> 1 Corinthians 12:7

David had a slingshot. I am certain thousands of young men his age also possessed slingshots. But David's slingshot was used for God in a world-changing way. His increased dependence upon God increased the anointing he experienced.

> *Anything common in you will become uncommon under the anointing.*

2. Anything common in you will become uncommon under the anointing.

The anointing on David's life made a common weapon an uncommon one. (See 1 Samuel 17:45-51.) Remember — the anointing is the power of God. It removes burdens and destroys yokes of bondage:

> *And it shall come to pass in that day, that his burden shall be taken away from off thy shoulder, and his yoke from off thy neck, and the yoke shall be destroyed because of the anointing.*
>
> Isaiah 10:27

3. You do not need the weapons of others:

> *So David prevailed over the Philistine with a sling and with a stone, and smote the Philistine, and slew him; but there was no sword in the hand of David.*
>
> 1 Samuel 17:50

4. Others will believe that your weapon is not sufficient to complete your Assignment:

> *And Saul armed David with his armour, and he put an helmet of brass upon his head; also he armed him with a coat of mail. And David girded his sword upon his armour, and he assayed to go; for he had not proved it.*
>
> 1 Samuel 17:38,39

5. You must refuse to copy, duplicate, or use the weapons other men use in their battles:

> *And David said unto Saul, I cannot go with these; for I have not proved them. And David put them off him.*
>
> 1 Samuel 17:39

6. Whatever you have been given will create anything else you have been promised.

   Moses possessed a rod:

> *And the Lord said unto him, What is that in thine hand? And he said, A rod. And he said, Cast it on the ground. And he cast it on the ground, and it became a serpent; and Moses fled from before it. And the Lord said unto Moses, Put forth thine hand, and take it by the tail. And he put forth his hand, and caught it, and it became a rod in his hand: that they may believe that the Lord God of their fathers, the God of Abraham, the God of Isaac, and the God of Jacob, hath appeared unto thee.*
>
> Exodus 4:2-5

7. You have something that makes you unique. So you must discern it. Develop it and build your life and ministry around the unique gift, strength, or talent God has given you. (See 1 Corinthians 12:14-21.) Do not build your life trying to correct your weaknesses. Build your life defining and refining the strengths and gifts God has given you. These strengths are the weapons God will use in warfare. These strengths are the vehicles to each victory.

8. God is already aware of your greatest fear and weakness. The Lord said something very interesting to Jeremiah when the prophet felt overwhelmed with his Assignment:

> *Then said I, Ah, Lord God! behold, I cannot speak: for I am a child.*
>
> Jeremiah 1:6

God corrected him concerning his obsession with his weakness:

> *But the LORD said unto me, Say not, I am a child: for thou shalt go to all that I shall send thee, and whatsoever I command thee thou shalt speak. Be not afraid of their faces: for I am with thee to deliver thee, saith the LORD.*
>
> Jeremiah 1:7,8
> (Also see 2 Timothy 1:7.)

9. God is not interested in what you cannot do. He is interested in whatever you are willing to do.

10. Your weakness will not stop your Assignment if your heart is right. Joseph lacked the social skills of becoming likable to his brothers. But he had another gift: the ability to interpret dreams. It was this ability that moved him from the prison into the palace. (See Genesis 41:39-45.)

11. Whatever you lack is of no concern when God chooses to bless you supernaturally. The widow of Zarephath did not have a job. She obviously had no social connections to offer people. In fact, she did not even have the appeal to unlock the giving of benevolent people. Her family was either dead, incapable, or uncaring. (See 1 Kings 17.)

12. Your respect for the anointing on others will increase the power of your own calling. But the widow of Zarephath did have the ability to listen to a man of God. And it was that strength that

kept her in abundant provision during the worst famine of her life. (See 1 Kings 17.)

13. You already possess everything you need to accomplish your present assignment. So inventory what you have been given. Document those persons with whom you have favor or access. List the marvelous and wonderful blessings of God that are already within your reach. (See Philippians 4:13,19.)

14. When you exhaust the benefits of your present season, you become qualified to enter your next season of increase. So be diligent to raise every inch of what you presently possess to its highest level of excellence. What you do first will always determine what God will allow you to do second. (See Matthew 6:33.)

15. Respect the Assignment of others. When you become appreciative of the gifts and strengths of others, favor will flow toward you like Niagara Falls. This is unexplainable and unstoppable. But what you respect will come toward you. And the anointing you appreciate, is the anointing that increases in your life. (See Ephesians 5:20.)

16. Acknowledge every good thing in you.

> *That the communication of our faith may become effectual by the acknowledging of every good thing which is in you in Christ Jesus.*
>
> Philemon 1:6

17. Expect your greatest strengths and gifts to improve, increase, and become perfected through the presence of the Holy Spirit in your life:

> *The Lord will perfect that which concerneth me....*
>
> Psalm 138:8

18. Expect your strengths and gifts to continue for the rest of eternity:

> *Being confident of this very thing, that he which hath begun a good work in you will perform it until the day of Jesus Christ.*
>
> Philippians 1:6

And never forget that your Assignment may cost you everything, because everything important, always costs. ALWAYS. But what you receive in return for your determined obedience will always astound you, because what God gives in return is HIMSELF.

> *For ye are bought with a price: therefore glorify God in your body, and in your spirit, which are God's.*
>
> 1 Corinthians 6:20

**Something you already hold in your hand will defeat any plan of your enemy.**

# Conclusion

I hope this book has helped you to recognize and pursue the Assignment God has waiting for you now. Thank you for giving me access to your life. It is not an accident that these burning truths and Wisdom Keys have now passed from my heart into your heart. God has connected us, my precious friend.

Now, go and succeed...BEYOND ANYTHING YOU HAVE EVER DREAMED BEFORE. Find that place He has reserved for you from the foundation of the world. Allow Him to use you as His serving vessel to bless the people of this earth. Fulfill your destiny. Discover and fulfill your Assignment.

# About the Author

The ministry of Dr. Mike Murdock is known around the world. Over twelve thousand audiences in thirty-six countries have been blessed in his crusades and Bible seminars. Mike is also a noted author, having written 77 books including the bestsellers, *Wisdom for Winning*, *Dream Seeds*, and *The Double Diamond Principle*. And he is an accomplished pianist, singer, and composer, with over 5,000 songs to his credit including, *I Am Blessed*, *You Can Make It*, and *Jesus, Just the Mention of Your Name*.

Dr. Murdock also hosts a television program, *Wisdom Keys With Mike Murdock*, which broadcasts weekly. And a radio program, *The Secret Place*, which broadcasts daily.

## Other Books by Mike Murdock

The Making of a Champion
The One-Minute Devotional
One-Minute Pocket Devotional for Business Professionals
One-Minute Pocket Devotional for Teens
One-Minute Pocket Devotional for Men
One-Minute Pocket Devotional for Women
One-Minute Businessman's Devotional
One-Minute Businesswoman's Devotional
The Businessman's Topical Bible
The Businesswoman's Topical Bible
The Father's Topical Bible
The Mother's Topical Bible
The Teens Topical Bible
Wisdom for Winning
Secrets for Winning at Work
Wisdom for Crisis Times
Dare to Succeed

To contact the author write:

Dr. Mike Murdock
Wisdom Training Center
P.O. Box  99
Dallas, TX 75221